Kids'
Book of Devotions

Also by Mark Littleton:

The Sports Heroes Series
  Baseball
  Football

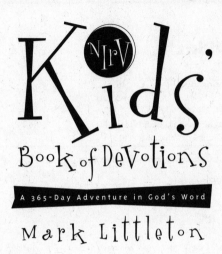

NIrV Kids' Book of Devotions

A 365-Day Adventure in God's Word

Mark Littleton

ZONDERVAN.com/
AUTHORTRACKER
follow your favorite authors

NIrV Kids' Book of Devotions
Copyright © 1998 by Mark Littleton

Requests for information should be addressed to:
Zonderkidz, *Grand Rapids, Michigan 49530*

Library of Congress Cataloging-in-Publication Data

Littleton, Mark R., 1950–
    NIrV kids' book of devotions : a 365-day adventure in God's Word / Mark Littleton.
       p. cm.
    Includes index.
    Summary: Presents daily devotional readings and prayers arranged by weekly themes covering such topics as friendship, school, sin, persecution, fear, love, trusting God, and more.
    ISBN: 0-310-22130-7 (pbk.)
    1. Children—Prayer—books and devotions—English. 2. Devotional calendars—Juvenile literature. [1. Prayer books and devotions. 2. Devotional calendars.] I. Title.
BV4571.2.L58 1998
242'.62-dc 21
                    98-22806
                         CIP
                         AC

Interior design by Sue Vandenberg Koppenol

Printed in the United States of America

10 11 12 13 14 /DCI/ 35 34 33

To my Tuesday Bible study group
Bill and Sue Ellen Radhe
Crissy Daniel
Len Nardozzi
Martie Armstrong
Bill Foss
Thanks for praying and hanging in there

Come to Me!

Come to me, all of you who are tired and are carrying heavy loads. I will give you rest.

MATTHEW 11:28

What do you do on your birthday? Eat cake. Play games. Open presents.

Yes, open presents. That's the most fun.

Think of God's Word as God's present to us. When we read and understand a verse, it's like opening a gift. Each verse is a special message of God's love to us. A little present!

The above text is one to memorize. What does it mean? If you're tired of trying to be good and obey the rules, stop. Come to Jesus, and he'll show you how!

That's a great gift, don't you think?

Father, thank you for your rest. Help me to learn to rest in you and to live by your peace. Amen.

THEME: THE BIBLE

How to Overcome Sin

I have hidden your word in my heart so that I won't sin against you.

PSALM 119:11

God's Word tells you how to avoid sin.

What is sin? It's anything that God says is evil and wrong. Hatred. Impatience. Stealing. Lying. You know what most sins are. But some of them are hard to overcome.

The verse above is a good way to beat sin. Look it up. Memorize it.

How does it work? When you "hide" God's Word in your heart, you put it deep and safe there. It's like something precious a friend said to you that you want to remember. When you treasure God's Word like that, you'll find you can fight sin better. Why? Because that's the way God made life! His Word is powerful!

Lord, let me treasure your Word. Lead me to dig deep and to find the great truths that will help me live well for you. In Jesus, amen.

THEME: THE BIBLE

What God's Word Does

God has breathed life into all of Scripture. It is useful for teaching us what is true. It is useful for correcting our mistakes. It is useful for making our lives whole again. It is useful for training us to do what is right.

2 TIMOTHY 3:16

Have you ever followed a trail in the woods? That can be scary if you don't know where it's going. But if you've traveled it many times, you know it's good. And you follow it with confidence.

The Bible says that God's Word is like a trail through the woods. Paul wrote in 2 Timothy 3:16 that it

teaches—shows us how to stay on God's trail
warns—points out when we get off his trail
corrects—helps us find the way back to the trail
and trains in right living—keeps us on the trail.

God's Word has that kind of power. Every time you read it, every time you hear it preached and read, listen for God's voice. Listen to what he's saying to you. And then go and obey it. Stick to God's trail and you'll get where he wants you to go.

Jesus, I want to hear your voice in your Word. Speak to me as I read and let me walk with you happily. Amen.

THEME: THE BIBLE

God's Word Is Like a Knife

The word of God is living and active. It is sharper than any sword that has two edges. It cuts deep enough to separate soul from spirit. It can separate joints from bones. It judges the thoughts and purposes of the heart.

HEBREWS 4:12

God's Word cuts deep.

Did you know that? It's like a knife.

Have you ever cut an apple in half? What happens when you do? The innermost seeds are exposed. You see what's inside.

That's what God's Word does in our hearts. It goes deep inside and shows us what's there. The verse in Hebrews that is written out above shows us the power of Scripture.

Have you ever sat in church and suddenly heard the preacher say something that made you feel like everyone knew what you'd done wrong? That's the Holy Spirit speaking to you through God's Word. The Spirit shows us what's inside our hearts.

Holy Spirit, speak to me in church and in your Word. I want to be like Jesus in every way. Through Jesus, amen.

THEME: THE BIBLE

God's Word Is Like a Seed

A farmer went out to plant his seed. He scattered the seed on the ground. Some fell on a path. Birds came and ate it up. Some seed fell on rocky places, where there wasn't much soil.

MATTHEW 13:3–4

Do you have a garden? Maybe not, but I'm sure you know how to make things grow.

First you plant the seeds. Then you water them. Then you wait.

God's Word is like a seed. In fact, Jesus told a story about a farmer who planted seeds. Some didn't grow at all. Some died young. Some were choked by weeds. And a few grew to bear fruit.

That's how God's Word works. A verse is a seed. You plant it deep in your heart. There you listen to it and talk to yourself about it. And soon it bears fruit in your life. What the Word says to do, you do!

That's the whole point of reading God's Word—to change your life.

Lord, I want you to change my life. Work in me and make me like Jesus. Amen.

THEME: THE BIBLE

A Lamp in the Darkness

Your word is like a lamp that shows me the way. It is like a light that guides me.

PSALM 119:105

Have you ever gone into a bathroom at night, turned on the light, and watched as some ugly bug disappeared down a drain? Yuck! Bugs don't like light. They scurry away. They want to stay in the dark. They don't want to be seen.

Did you know God's Word is like that light? In the passage above we can see how it works. When God switches his Word on in our lives, we sometimes see things we don't want to see. Lying. Stealing. Not studying in school. Making jokes about God's truth. They're the bugs of sin God wants to show to us. After we see them in the light, we can get rid of them once and for all.

Father, let me walk in the light of life. Show me any sins that I've done and help me stop doing them. In Jesus, amen.

THEME: THE BIBLE

God's Word Is Alive

I take delight in your orders. I won't fail to obey your word.

PSALM 119:16

Take a breath.

Ah! Did that feel good?

Now breathe on something—a candle flame, a leaf. What happens? Does it move around? Does it become "alive"?

Did you know that the Bible says God's Word has God's breath in it? In 2 Timothy 3:16, Paul says, "God has breathed life into all of Scripture." In other words, the Bible has the very breath of God inside it.

What does that mean? Just this: when you read the Bible, you're reading something that has life. Other words and sayings are just that: words and sayings. But God's Word is alive.

Next time you read some of it, see if it moves inside of you!

Lord Jesus, you say your Word is alive. Let it live in me. Amen.

God Is My Shepherd

The LORD is my shepherd. He gives me everything I need.
PSALM 23:1

Why do we go to church?

Is it to hear a sermon? Is it to sing some songs? Is it to worship God?

All these things. But there's something else you may have missed. Remember the 23rd Psalm. The first verse is quoted above.

God is a shepherd. Jesus was called the Good Shepherd. And the leaders, pastors, elders, and deacons in a church are "undershepherds." They're under Jesus. Jesus is the boss. They're his servants.

And who do they serve? Not just him, but us. They help us not be "in want." They show us the green pastures of truth and friendship. They lead us to the quiet waters of fellowship and good character. And they guide us in the right paths.

Church is God's way of helping you make it as a Christian.

Holy God, let me learn in church and Sunday school. Open my eyes so I may see your good truths. Amen.

THEME: THE CHURCH

Stir Up One Another

Let us consider how we can stir up one another to love. Let us help one another to do good works.

HEBREWS 10:24

A boy said in class, "When I grow up, I'm not gonna go to church."

The teacher asked him why. He said, "Because it's so boring."

The teacher then said, "You want to know how to make it not boring?"

His eyes lit up. "How?"

They talked about this verse in Hebrews about stirring up one another. The teacher said, "When you come to church, try to think of all the ways you can encourage your friends to show love and do good."

He was amazed. "That's what I'm supposed to do here?"

"Sure," his teacher answered. "And a lot of other things. But that's a big one."

Later on, he helped a younger girl read a verse. When he smiled, the teacher winked. There was a boy learning how to make church a great time every Sunday.

Eternal God, help me to be an encourager. Show me someone today I can encourage with your Word. Amen.

THEME: THE CHURCH

Parts of a Body

The body is not made up of just one part. It has many parts. Suppose the foot says, "I am not a hand. So I don't belong to the body." It is still part of the body.

1 CORINTHIANS 12:14–15

Have you ever thought of what you might do if you were blind? Or deaf? Or were missing your legs?

It would be tough, but many people live with such problems and do fine.

There's one person, though, that God never wants to be handicapped. Do you know who that person is? Jesus' body, the church.

Yes, we're called Jesus' body in the Bible. He is the head, and we're the hands, feet, eyes, ears, liver, and heart. That's why Jesus needs everyone to take a role and play a part. You may be a spleen, or a big toe, or a whole hand. But when you don't participate, you're handicapping the church.

See what Paul told the Corinthians in the above verse? How do you get the most out of church? By doing something. By being a part. By giving of yourself.

Perfect Lord, show me my place in your church. Help me to find a ministry or do something that builds up others. In Jesus' name, amen.

THEME: THE CHURCH

Share!

Share with God's people who are in need.

ROMANS 12:13

A boy went by a pet store and stared at the puppies in the window. Each day he came and watched them grow. One day, he walked in and pulled out his wallet. "I want to buy a puppy," he told the clerk.

"Which one?" the clerk asked.

The boy pointed out the puppy he wanted.

"Oh, no," said the clerk. "I'm going to put that one to sleep. It has a bad leg. You can see that, can't you?"

The boy nodded. Then he pulled up his pant legs to reveal two braces on his feet and shins. "I want that puppy," he said with a smile, "because I know what it's like to have a bad leg, and I'll be a good friend to him."

What that boy did for the puppy is what we do for each other in the church. We share our lives and help each other when we're in need. So we're never alone!

My Father, help me to look out for hurting people. Show me a way to speak a comforting word to someone in trouble today. Amen.

THEME: THE CHURCH

What About That Pinky Finger?

If one part suffers, every part suffers with it. If one part is honored, every part shares in its joy.

1 CORINTHIANS 12:26

Sometimes I look at my pinky finger and think, "What good are you?" It doesn't seem to do much. But when I'm typing away on my computer, that pinky finger does a lot of jobs. It hits the A and the Q and the Z on my left, and the P, the quotation mark, and the slash on my right.

One day, I smashed my pinky finger with a hammer. Yow! That hurt. And you know what? I couldn't type worth beans. Every time I touched that pinky to a key, I went, "Yow!" I protected that pinky like nothing else. I didn't let anyone get near it.

Did you know that's the way we're to be in the church? See what Paul said in the verse from 1 Corinthians above? He meant that when anyone in the church hurts, we all hurt. And when anyone gets blessed, we're all blessed.

Next time you see someone hurting, tell him, "I'll protect you with a little prayer."

Lord, today I want to pray for _____. They're having a hard time. Help them, I pray, in Jesus' name, amen.

THEME: THE CHURCH

Be Devoted!

Love each other deeply. Honor others more than your-selves.

ROMANS 12:10

At one time I had a dog named Jacques. He was a big poodle, not one of those little dinky ones with jeweled collars. He was as big as a Lab or a German Shepherd.

You know the thing I liked most about Jacques? Every day when I came home from school, he ran to greet me at the door. He barked with joy. He jumped up and down, fetched his ball, rolled over, and made a regular fool of himself.

Did you ever realize that's how we're to treat others in the church? We're to be so glad to see them, we smile, we hug, we speak encouraging words. Paul said it that way in the verse above. "Love each other deeply!"

Couldn't you use some people in your life like that? People who are devoted to you? That's how God wants his church to be—all of us devoted to each other. Can you imagine how it would be to go to a place like that every Sunday?

Spirit of God, I want to be devoted to others the way you tell us. Lead me in that way. In Jesus, amen.

THEME: THE CHURCH

Get Taught How to Live

Don't be wise in your own eyes. Have respect for the LORD and avoid evil. That will bring health to your body. It will make your bones strong.

PROVERBS 3:7–8

You know what I hated about church growing up? They always seemed to be telling me how I should live. I wanted to do things my way, but the church said, "Do it God's way." I wanted to go off and have fun, but the church said, "Listen to God and his Word." I wanted to make friends with people with bad character. The church said, "Be careful what friends you make. They could lead you astray."

At the time, I didn't like it. But after I became a Christian I saw the wisdom of learning right from wrong. Do you want to know how to live right, clean, happy, and whole? How do you learn those things? By going to a place where they teach you all about it. And what is that place? Church.

Father, let me be a learner. Let me listen and obey the things I learn in church so that I can please you always. Amen.

THEME: THE CHURCH

Real Fellowship

Let us not give up meeting together. Some are in the habit of doing this. Instead, let us cheer each other up with words of hope. Let us do it all the more as you see the day coming when Christ will return.

HEBREWS 10:25

If you've gone to church much, you know something they're always talking about: fellowship. "Let's have some fellowship this Sunday," the pastor says, and what do they do? They have cookies and coffee and juice in where? Fellowship Hall, of course.

Well, that's part of it—being together, talking, joking, telling stories. But there's much more to it than just being friendly to each other.

Look at how it's stated in the Hebrews passage above. Fellowship is meeting together, sharing the Word of God, encouraging and helping each other, serving, giving, and loving. One of the best things about being a Christian is you know you have a lot of people who are praying for you, who are supporting you, who are on your side. And that's fellowship.

I want to fellowship the way you say, Lord, so help me give to others the way you give to me. Amen.

THEME: FELLOWSHIP

Let Me Be Me!

Christ has accepted you. So accept one another in order to bring praise to God.

ROMANS 15:7

How do you treat other Christians when you fellowship with them? One way is simply to accept them. That's what Paul said in Romans 15:7.

I remember when I first became a Christian and I went to a pastor to offer my help at church. I was nervous about it because I didn't know how he'd react to my past. I'd been a hippie, used drugs, gotten drunk, and done a lot of bad things. But when I met with him and told him my story, he just listened. At the end, he said, "Mark, you're welcome here to do anything and everything you want. We'd love to have you come fellowship with us every Sunday."

I was amazed. Had he heard me right? Yes, he had. And he accepted me as I was, nothing held back. That's fellowship.

Make me a listener to others, Lord. Open my ears so I can hear what people are really saying to me. Amen.

THEME: FELLOWSHIP

Give Some Applause

Honor others more than yourselves.

ROMANS 12:10

At our church talent show, the acts were great. The organizer did a tremendous job. When she came on to thank everyone at the end, the crowd cheered and cheered. But when the cheering stopped, she said, "I want to thank the different participants here. They all worked so hard on these songs and skits, and we didn't think we could pull it off. But everyone did. Without them, it would never have worked."

Everyone clapped again. When the talent show was over, though, I thought of the verse above quoted from Romans. "Honor each other." That is exactly what that organizer had done.

When we honor others, we show we care about them, love them, want them to be praised. And that's a prime ingredient of what happens in true fellowship.

Father, I want to honor your people. Who can I honor today in a special way? Show me, and I will. In Jesus' name, amen.

THEME: FELLOWSHIP

Take Off Those Shoes and Socks

You were chosen to be free. But don't use your freedom as an excuse to live in sin. Instead, serve one another in love.
GALATIANS 5:13

The youth club didn't like the idea, but we decided to go with it. Everyone divided into pairs. Then one member of each pair sat on a chair and took off his shoes and socks.

"Oh, yuck!"

"Smell those bananas, man. Whew!"

But after everyone had his say, we did it. Everyone washed each other's feet, just like Jesus did in John 13. Why did we do this? To serve one another. Like it says in Galatians 5:13, "Serve one another in love."

Washing each other's feet was a symbol of something we're supposed to do every day. Help out. Give a hand. Share a dollar. Cook a meal. Go to the nursing home and read a story.

Service not only makes for real fellowship, it also creates fun. After all, how many times since that night have we laughed about those stinky feet?

Jesus, I know you were trying to teach us something great when you washed the disciples' feet. Help me to serve others today. Amen.

THEME: FELLOWSHIP

Wash It Away

Be kind and tender to one another. Forgive each other, just as God forgave you because of what Christ has done.

EPHESIANS 4:32

My daughter had lied about her homework. She wanted to play with her friend, Jennifer, so she told me that she'd finished her homework. But she hadn't done anything.

We finally got a call from her teacher. "She's not bringing in her homework, and she's getting zeroes on everything," Mrs. Altman said.

I was angry. I wanted to spank her. But when we sat down to talk, she admitted she had lied. Then she said, "Will you forgive me, Daddy?"

My heart melted. I thought about forgiving as Jesus forgave us. Jesus forgave me for all sorts of things; I could certainly forgive my daughter.

I hugged her and told her not to do it again. Forgiving is hard sometimes, but it builds love. Whom do you need to forgive?

Forgive me, loving Father, for all the things I've done wrong this week. I especially feel bad about _____. Cleanse my heart, I pray, in Jesus, amen.

THEME: FELLOWSHIP

Let Me Show You How

So cheer each other up with the hope you have. Build each other up. In fact, that's what you are doing.

1 THESSALONIANS 5:11

My Little League coach yelled, "Go in there and hit it out of the park, Mark." But this pitcher was a fire-baller, and wild. I was terrified. Getting hit by his fastball was a fast trip to Painsville.

Every pitch he threw, I flinched, stepped back, swung wild, and missed. I struck out.

At the next practice, the coach took me out to the diamond and said, "Look, I'll show you how to hit those kinds of pitches." He worked with me, pitching hard and showing me how not to flinch. Eventually, I learned to hit even off those fireballers.

That coach's help reminds me of this verse in 1 Thessalonians 5:11: "Cheer each other up"!

Encouragement is much more than a nice word; it's showing a person how. It's helping them learn. It's getting in the dirt and swinging for them.

Can you do that with your friends?

Perfect Master, let me encourage one person today in school. Show me someone who needs an encouraging word, for Jesus' sake, amen.

THEME: FELLOWSHIP

Love Deeply

Have an honest and true love for your brothers and sisters. Love each other deeply, from the heart.

1 PETER 1:22

A little girl needed a special kind of blood to live. One of the few people who could supply her type was her little brother. Finally, after much talk and persuasion, he agreed. As the nurse poked the needle in his arm to draw the blood, he lay back and closed his eyes. Finally, he asked, "When will I die?"

The nurse was astounded. "I'm just taking your blood, honey."

The boy's eyes grew big. "You mean I won't die?"

"Of course not."

He had thought by giving his sister blood, he was giving up his life for her.

Now that's love, the kind of love Peter spoke about when he said, "Love each other deeply, from the heart" (1 Peter 1:22). And that's the kind of love that makes Christian fellowship sweet and beautiful.

What kind of love are you showing others today?

I know I should love others, Lord, but sometimes I just don't like people. Help me to change for the good. Amen.

THEME: FELLOWSHIP

Choking on the Gospel

I am not ashamed of the good news. It is God's power. And it will save everyone who believes.

ROMANS 1:16

One day, Jenny sat by Dawn on the bus. Jenny turned to Dawn and said, "Someone told me you go to church."

Dawn was embarrassed. So she said, "My mom and dad make me go."

"Oh, so you're not really a Christian, then?" Jenny asked.

"Well, yeah, I'm a Christian, but . . ."

"But you're not really into it?"

"I guess."

Afterwards, Dawn felt horrible. She had just experienced something every Christian goes through: being embarrassed that you go to church, or that you're a Christian.

In Romans 1:16, Paul said he wasn't ashamed of the gospel. How does that compare to Dawn's attitude? How about your attitude?

Jesus, sometimes I'm embarrassed to tell other kids I go to church. Help me not to feel that way and to become bold in telling about Jesus. Amen.

THEME: EVANGELISM

Power from Above

You will receive power when the Holy Spirit comes on you. Then you will be my witnesses in Jerusalem. You will be my witnesses in all Judea and Samaria. And you will be my witnesses from one end of the earth to the other.

ACTS 1:8

Yesterday, Dawn was put on the spot and felt bad about her witness for Jesus. How can we as Christians be fearless and bold, like the first Christians?

There's only one way: when we're strengthened by God's Spirit in us. Before he ascended into heaven, Jesus promised his disciples spiritual power.

To be a "witness" is to tell others what we have seen in the Bible, in church, and in Jesus. Many Christians are afraid to do this. They're afraid they'll be laughed at, or hated, or even persecuted. But the Holy Spirit will give you power to stand up to anyone if you ask him. The first thing to do in sharing the gospel with your friends is to ask the Spirit to empower you.

When you do that, you have all the strength of God on your side. And you won't be ashamed like Dawn.

I want to be a witness, Master. Show me how, for Jesus, amen.

THEME: EVANGELISM

What to Tell Them

What I received I passed on to you. And it is the most important of all. Here is what it is. Christ died for our sins, just as Scripture said he would. He was buried. He was raised from the dead on the third day.

1 CORINTHIANS 15:3–4

Okay, you're not ashamed of being a Christian. You just don't know what to tell others.

First Corinthians 15:3–4 records what the apostle Paul told people: "Christ died for our sins, he was buried, and he was raised on the third day."

The gospel is very simple, so simple that many people think it can't be true. But in a nutshell, it's three things:

1. We are sinners.
2. Christ died for our sins.
3. He rose again to prove his power over sin and death.

The only other thing to ask is: Do you believe this? If you do, you're a Christian!

My Lord, help me to learn to witness to others. Teach me the verses and help me to use them to speak. In Jesus' name, amen.

THEME: EVANGELISM

The Knock on Your Door

Some people did accept him. They believed in his name. He gave them the right to become children of God.

JOHN 1:12

One day you hear a knock at the door. You and your friend Josh open the door, and there stands a man in a white robe. His hands are scarred. His brow looks cut. But he's smiling. He says, "I'm Jesus. I died for your sins. Will you let me come in and be your friend?"

You look at Josh, and he says, "This must be a joke."

"No," Jesus says, "I'm for real. Will you be my friends and come follow me? I promise, I'll give you eternal life, and I'll never let you down."

Josh snorts and laughs, but you stand there. What do you do?

In the book of John, it says that all who receive Jesus into their hearts become children of God (John 1:12). The above story is a picture of receiving Jesus. It's like inviting him into your house, into your school, onto your playground. When you do that, you receive him. And that's what it means to be a Christian.

Have you done that?

Lord, I believe in you and I want to follow you. Show me how to walk in your steps. Amen.

THEME: EVANGELISM

Salvation in No One Else

You can't be saved by believing in anyone else. God has given us no other name under heaven that will save us.
ACTS 4:12

Tim, Rasheed, Hiroyuki, and Samed sat on the bench waiting to go up to bat. Rasheed suddenly said, "Do you guys have religions that you believe?"

"Sure," Hiroyuki said. "I'm a Buddhist. We believe in the teachings of Buddha."

"And I'm a Hindu," Samed answered. "We follow many gods."

Rasheed said, "I'm a Muslim. We worship Allah."

Everyone turned to Tim. He said quietly, "I'm a Christian. We follow Jesus."

"Every way is okay," Samed said. "They all end up at the same place."

Everyone else agreed. But Tim went home troubled. When he talked to his dad that night, his dad opened up to this verse in Acts 4:12. The verse referred to Jesus.

What does this verse say to you about Jesus and other religions? What might Tim tell his friends tomorrow?

Father, I know kids who believe other religions. Help me to understand them and love them too, but also to tell them the truth. Amen.

THEME: EVANGELISM

Give a Straight But Gentle Answer

But make sure in your hearts that Christ is Lord. Always be ready to give an answer to anyone who asks you about the hope you have. Be ready to give the reason for it. But do it gently and with respect.

1 PETER 3:15

Tim was in a tough spot. Nobody likes to be told they're wrong, and especially that their religion is wrong. People get very angry when Christians say that. But what else can we say? Isn't Jesus the only one who died for our sins? Buddha didn't. Neither did Muhammad.

How might Tim approach his friends about this? Peter gave us good advice in 1 Peter 3:15. He advised both gentleness and respect.

That's the key. Tell your friends about Jesus. Tell them how you became a Christian. Don't agree that other religions are true. But respect their views and don't belittle them.

That's a good start. Do you think you can do that?

Jesus, sometimes I'm not so gentle on others. Help me to learn to be respectful. Amen.

THEME: EVANGELISM

The Bottom Line

Believe in the Lord Jesus. Then you and your family will be saved.

ACTS 16:31

"All I want to know is what I should do," the young man said to me. "Get it down to the most basic thing."

My friend wanted to become a Christian, but he found a lot of the things I told him confusing. I showed him verse after verse. He just didn't seem to understand. I was also getting frustrated.

My friend finally said, "Okay, what's the bottom line? Where do I start?"

I remembered a verse I memorized long ago. I opened my Bible to Acts 16:31 where Paul told a jailer what to do to be saved. Paul said, "Believe in the Lord Jesus. Then you and your family will be saved" (Acts 16:31).

That's the gospel. It's that simple. Believe in Jesus. Anyone can do that, if they wish.

Perhaps you might memorize that verse and many of the others in this book. Remember the Word of God has the power. You just need to point your friends to it and let it do its work.

All-powerful God, help me to trust that you will work when I speak the truth to others. In Jesus, amen.

THEME: EVANGELISM

Pray First

Those who are led by the Spirit of God are children of God.
ROMANS 8:14

Every Christian sooner or later wants God to tell them what they should do—either in a situation, or for something at school, or even for their life's work.

But how do you know what God wants you to do?

Simple. Paul said, "Those who are led by the Spirit of God are children of God" (Romans 8:14). If you're a child of God, then the Spirit of God will lead you. How?

One day, my daughter and I were fixing the door in her room. As I took it out of its slots, a spring popped out. We couldn't find it, though we looked everywhere. Without that spring, I couldn't fix the door. Then I stopped and thought. Why hadn't I prayed about it? I did at that moment, and a second later, Alisha said, "Is this what you're looking for?"

It was the spring.

One way to find out something from God is to ask him. Pray.

Show me how to pray, Lord, so that I can be a kid who prays about everything. In Jesus' name, amen.

THEME: GOD'S WILL

Tested by a Test

How can young people keep their lives pure? By living in keeping with your word.

PSALM 119:9

Terry came home from school rather upset. His mom noticed his downcast looks and asked him what was wrong. "They want me to lie about a test," Terry told her. Soon, the story came out. Several boys cheated by copying Terry's paper. Now they wanted him to lie to the teacher about it.

His mother asked him, "And you don't know what to do?"

"I don't want to hurt my friends," Terry said. "But I also don't want to lie."

She opened his Bible to Psalm 119:9. Then she said, "You will do the right thing if you obey God's Word."

"And that means not lie?"

"Yes," his mom answered. "And maybe you also need to tell your friends to own up to the truth."

Many of life's situations are tough to work out. But if you use God's Word, God promises you'll please him.

Right now, Jesus, I have a tough situation with _____. Show me what's right and help me to do it. In Jesus' name, amen.

THEME: GOD'S WILL

When You Want Something But Can't Have It

So I say, live by the Holy Spirit's power. Then you will not do what your sinful nature wants you to do.

GALATIANS 5:16

Madeline and Tina stared at the money in Tina's hand. Fifty cents. The ice-cream cones they wanted were fifty cents each. Madeline thought Tina should give her the cone since she'd paid for them both last time. But Tina wanted that cone, too.

As she thought about what to do, Tina remembered what she'd learned in Sunday school. Her flesh wanted that cone, but she knew that was selfish. She said, "Okay, here's the money."

But suddenly Madeline said, "Hey, look, we can get two Pop-Ices for the same amount. Let's do that."

That often happens when you go with God. Do the right thing, and he makes it possible for everyone to share.

I know, Father, you will show me the right way if I'll seek it. But sometimes I don't want to seek it. Change me on the inside, Lord, about this. Amen.

THEME: GOD'S WILL

No Answers

There is one thing we can be sure of when we come to God in prayer. If we ask anything in keeping with what he wants, he hears us.

1 John 5:14

"I pray," Jeff said, "but I never get any answers."

Mr. Clime opened his Bible and showed Jeff 1 John 5:14. Then Mr. Clime said, "When you pray according to God's will, he always hears and answers."

"But how do I know what his will is?"

"This," said Mr. Clime, holding up a Bible. "Just find out what God says about what you need or desire, and then pray according to it."

"You mean if I want a puppy for Christmas, I'll get one?"

"No, but what if you find a verse that says, 'In everything give thanks'? Then you could pray, 'God, let me be thankful for whatever happens.' And God would answer."

If you want to know God's will, just open your Bible. It's all in the book.

Eternal Lord, sometimes I just don't want to know your will because I'll have to do it. Change me in this area. In Jesus, amen.

THEME: GOD'S WILL

The Will of God for us

God wants you to be made holy.

1 THESSALONIANS 4:3

What does God most want for us? First Thessalonians 4:3 reveals the answer: "God wants you to be made holy." That's a big word, but it means "holiness," or to be "used only for the things of God."

In other words, God wants each of us to live holy lives, to do those things that please him. Here's a little chart. One side is what we might like to do. The other is God's way. Which will you choose?

Our Way	**God's Way**
1. Cheating on a test and getting an A.	1. Flunking because we didn't study, and then promising to do better.
2. Using foul language.	2. Avoiding foul language.
3. Lying.	3. Admitting what you did wrong.
4. Stealing.	4. Paying back what you took.

Which do you think will gain God's blessing?

Father, there are things I've done wrong. You know what they are. Help me to make them right. Amen.

What Does God Want?

Don't live any longer the way this world lives. Let your way of thinking be completely changed. Then you will be able to test what God wants for you. And you will agree that what he wants is right.

ROMANS 12:2

"What does God want from me anyway?" complained Darla. "I try to do what I think he wants, and then I do it all wrong."

This is a common complaint. No matter how well you obey, sooner or later you flub up.

Romans 12:2 helps. When it says, "Let your way of thinking be completely changed," it means "made new inside and out." That way, you will prove God's will is the best way. How are you made new? Well, how do you make grass grow on bald soil? You water it and nourish it.

In the same way, water and nourish your mind with the things of God—the Word, prayer, helping, serving, giving—and you will grow good, green spiritual grass in your life.

Help me, Master, to nourish my heart in your Word. That way I'll always be sure of what you want from me. Amen.

THEME: GOD'S WILL

Keep in Step

Since we live by the Spirit, let us march in step with the Spirit.

GALATIANS 5:25

A boy followed his father down the beach. He tried to step in his father's footprints. But his father's stride was too long, and the boy had to jump to reach the prints. When he jumped, he sometimes slipped and fell over.

How could that boy walk in his father's footsteps? By asking his father to take smaller steps!

Galatians 5:25 says we should "march in step with the Spirit." When God makes us his child, he doesn't expect us to get all grown up in a week, or even a year. The Spirit tailors his stride to our ability.

What does that mean? It means that God will help you grow in faith at a pace you can keep up with. You just need to trust him and believe that he's leading you where you need to go.

I want to walk in your footsteps, Jesus. Show me how so I can please you. In your name, amen.

THEME: GOD'S WILL

Final Exams

Watch and pray. Then you won't fall into sin when you are tempted. The spirit is willing. But the body is weak.

MARK 14:38

The word *tempt* means "to test or try." Teachers use tests to find out whether you know the facts. A temptation is Satan's way of finding out whether you will obey God or not.

When Satan tested Job to see whether he would fail the faith test, he also tempted Job to curse God. When Satan tempted Jesus in the wilderness, he devised three tests he hoped Jesus would fail.

Satan will tempt you all the time. Lying, stealing, cheating, cursing, hating, being jealous, getting angry without cause—all these are his tricks of the trade. How do you beat such temptations?

Jesus' advice in Mark 14:38 is helpful. He says two things: Watch. Pray. Two ways to beat the devil at his own games.

Lord Jesus, show me how to watch and pray so that I can defeat the devil. Amen.

THEME: TEMPTATION

The Fun Side of Temptation

My brothers and sisters, you will face all kinds of trouble. When you do, think of it as pure joy. Your faith will be put to the test. You know that when that happens it will produce in you the strength to continue.

JAMES 1:2–3

Have you ever thought of a temptation as being fun?

It can be. When you defeat the devil, he runs howling with rage. And you can snicker a little if you want. But he'll be back.

Maybe *fun* isn't the right word. Try *joy*. As James advised, "When you face trouble, think of it as pure joy."

Yes, you can consider all those times when you want to disobey or run or do something wrong as joy. It's a chance to show God what you're made of. It's also a chance to learn to persevere. That's a big word that means "hang in there."

So are you hanging in there today?

I don't want to give up, Lord. Show me how to hang in there like today's devotional says. In Jesus' name, amen.

THEME: TEMPTATION

How Not to Give In

You are tempted in the same way all other human beings are. God is faithful. He will not let you be tempted any more than you can take. But when you are tempted, God will give you a way out so that you can stand up under it.

1 CORINTHIANS 10:13

"It just gets me every time," complained Will.

"Why do you give in?" asked his dad.

"Because it's so much easier than standing up to it."

"But in the end you feel bad, and sometimes you get punished."

"Yeah." Will hung his head.

Will's problem is common. It's so much easier to give in to anger or hatred or arguing. But God promises us something. Paul tells us in 1 Corinthians 10:13 that what we're going through is common for all people. But God is faithful and will not let us be tempted beyond our powers. Instead, he will provide the way of escape. It might be simply turning and running. It might be quoting a Scripture. Or praying. But look for it. God promises the escape hatch is there.

Today I'm struggling with _____, Jesus. Help me to find the way of escape I know you've provided. Amen.

THEME: TEMPTATION

Does God Ever Tempt Us?

When you are tempted, you shouldn't say, "God is tempting me." God can't be tempted by evil. And he doesn't tempt anyone. But your own evil longings tempt you. They lead you on and drag you away.

JAMES 1:13–14

"The devil made me do it" is one way people claim they lose to temptation.

Another way is to say, "God let me down. He didn't help." Or, "God set me up. I walked into a trap."

Would God ever set you up? Or tempt you?

Never! James said that God never tempts us. He can never be tempted to do evil, either. No, when we're tempted, it's our evil desires that get in the way. When they get flowing, temptation is more difficult.

You can't blame your failures on God. But you can count on him to help, if you ask. Do you ask for his help when you're tempted? If not, try it today.

Perfect Friend, let me not give in to temptation today. I may want to, but I trust you to work in me not to want to. Amen.

THEME: TEMPTATION

What If ...?

Keep us from falling into sin when we are tempted. Save us from the evil one.

MATTHEW 6:13

"What if I just can't stand it any longer?" Billy asked. "Is it okay to give in then?"

Temptation is tricky. It comes in all kinds of disguises. Just when you've overcome one, another one jumps up and smacks you upside the head.

But Jesus had a remedy. When his disciples asked him to teach them to pray, he taught them the Lord's Prayer. You probably know it. It contains this line: "Keep us from falling into sin when we are tempted. Save us from the evil one" (Matthew 6:13).

"Keep us from falling into sin" means, "Don't let us fall into circumstances we can't overcome." When you pray that prayer, you're doing a wise thing: you're asking God to plan your way and make sure whatever tricks the devil throws at you, you can beat.

God will deliver you. Ask, Jesus said, and you shall receive.

I'm having trouble with this problem, Lord: _____. Help me to trust you to show me the way around or over it. In Jesus' name, amen.

THEME: TEMPTATION

God to the Rescue

So the Lord knows how to keep godly people safe in times of testing. He also knows how to keep ungodly people under guard until the day they will be judged.

2 PETER 2:9

"It was amazing," Tom said. "One minute I was about to yell at my sister. And then my dog popped up and licked her face. I laughed so hard, I forgot to be angry at her."

Yes, sometimes God uses the most amazing means to help us out of a tight spot. But he did promise to do this. Look at 2 Peter 2:9: "So the Lord knows how to keep godly people safe in times of testing."

God can "rescue" you from temptations and trials. That means he'll do something to stop them, like snuffing out a fire. Or he'll show you an escape route. Or he'll just give you strength to stand strong.

Do you need a rescue? Then call on the greatest Rescuer of them all.

I need rescuing, Father. I keep trying to defeat this sin, but it gets me every time. Show me the way out, I pray. In Jesus' name, amen.

THEME: TEMPTATION

If You Do Fall, Do This

God is faithful and fair. If we admit that we have sinned, he will forgive us our sins. He will forgive every wrong thing we have done. He will make us pure.

1 JOHN 1:9

Okay, you know God can help you when you're tempted. But what if you fail? What about when you do give in?

John had a ready answer in 1 John 1:9: "God is faithful and fair. If we admit that we have sinned, he will forgive us our sins. He will forgive every wrong thing we have done. He will make us pure."

When we fail, we simply need to admit or "confess" our sin. That means to "agree with God that what we did was wrong." It also means we tell the Lord we don't intend to do the sin again.

What happens then? God forgives us and purifies us from everything that was wrong. Even the stuff we didn't mention, or didn't know about.

No matter which way you go—win or lose—God is on your side. Trust him and he'll get you through.

Forgive me, God, for my giving in to sin today. And lead me in the way that is right. Amen.

THEME: TEMPTATION

A Great Man?

You should think in the same way Christ Jesus does. In his very nature he was God. But he did not think that being equal with God was something he should hold on to. Instead, he made himself nothing. He took on the very nature of a servant. He was made in human form.

PHILIPPIANS 2:5–7

"I just believe Jesus was a great man, that's all," Harrison said.

Quietly, Dave said, "You're wrong. He was God in human flesh."

"Get out of here!" Harrison cried. "How do you know that?"

Dave showed him Philippians 2:5–7. "Jesus was God," Dave explained. "But he didn't hold onto that right and position. Instead, he became a man, a servant. And he obeyed God, even when it meant that he had to die.

"Whether you like it or not," Dave concluded, "that's what the Bible teaches. We just have to deal with it."

Who do you believe Jesus was?

Father, I believe Jesus was your Son and he came to save me. Help me to stay strong in that belief always. Amen.

THEME: JESUS

What Jesus Said About Himself

Jesus said to them, "My Father is always doing his work. He is working right up to this very day. I am working too." For this reason, the Jews tried even harder to kill him. Jesus was not only breaking the Sabbath. He was even calling God his own Father. He was making himself equal with God.

JOHN 5:17–18

After hearing Dave, Harrison said, "But that wasn't what Jesus said. That was what others said about him. I'd like to hear what Jesus himself said."

"Easy," Dave answered. He flipped to John 5:17–18. What happened here? Jesus claimed God was his Father. When Jesus said this, he knew exactly what the response would be. For long ago God had told the Jews not to call God their personal Father. So when Jesus called God his father, the Jews wanted to stone him. Jesus was claiming to be equal with God the Father. If he's equal, he's God, too.

How much clearer could it be? Jesus said he was God. And Jesus was God!

I understand Jesus was God the Son in human form, Lord, so help me tell others this truth in gentleness and respect. Amen.

THEME: JESUS

God in Human Flesh

The high priest asked him, "Are you the Christ? Are you the Son of the Blessed One?" "I am," said Jesus. "And you will see the Son of Man sitting at the right hand of the Mighty One. You will see the Son of Man coming on the clouds of heaven." The high priest tore his clothes. "Why do we need any more witnesses?" he asked. "You have heard him say a very evil thing against God. What do you think?"

MARK 14:61–64

"Okay," Harrison answered. "I get that Jesus was sort of claiming to be equal to God. But that doesn't make him God in human flesh."

"Okay," Dave answered, "try this verse." He turned to the passage above and read how the high priest questioned Jesus about his identity. Was he really the Christ, the Messiah, the Son of God, God incarnate, God made in human flesh? What did Jesus answer? "I am."

When he heard Jesus' answer, the high priest tore his clothes. In the eyes of the Jews, it was blasphemy to claim to be God. That was precisely what Jesus did here. He claimed to be God incarnate—in human flesh.

Are you convinced?

My friends have questions, Father, when I tell them about Jesus. What do I say? Show me the words. Amen.

THEME: JESUS

Completely Human

There is only one God. And there is only one go-between for God and human beings. He is the man Christ Jesus.

1 TIMOTHY 2:5

"Well, if Jesus was God," Harrison said, "then he wasn't anything like us. So why should I trust him? He doesn't know what it's like to be me."

Dave thought about it, then said, "Here's something else the Bible says: 'There is only one God. And there is only one go-between for God and human beings. He is the man Christ Jesus'" (1 Timothy 2:5). Dave added, "Jesus was both completely God and completely human. My pastor says that's how he could die for our sins. Because he was a man, he could die for a man. Because he was God, he could die for everyone."

Harrison rubbed his chin. "But if this is true, why do so many people not believe it?"

Dave shook his head. "When you look at what the Bible says, you can't avoid it. I guess people just don't want to believe."

Do you want to believe?

Let me love those who reject Jesus, Master, so that I may continue to reach out to them. In Jesus, amen.

THEME: JESUS

Jesus Knows What It's Like

We have a high priest who can feel it when we are weak and hurting. We have a high priest who has been tempted in every way, just as we are. But he did not sin.

HEBREWS 4:15

"You mean Jesus really knows what it's like to be me?" Harrison exclaimed.

Dave grinned. "Yeah. Look at this verse: 'We have a high priest who can feel it when we are weak and hurting. We have a high priest who has been tempted in every way, just as we are. But he did not sin' (Hebrews 4:15). Jesus knows what it's like to be completely human. He faced every temptation we'll ever face, but he never gave in."

"That's it then," Harrison said. "He doesn't know what it's like to give in to temptation."

Everyone had a good laugh over that one. But then Dave said, "If Jesus ever did give into temptation, he couldn't die for our sins. He'd have to die for his own sins. And then where would we be?"

"Lost forever, I guess," Harrison said.

Thank you, Eternal God, that Jesus died for me. I hope I never forget his great love. In Jesus' name, amen.

THEME: JESUS

What Jesus Came to Give

Come to me, all of you who are tired and are carrying heavy loads. I will give you rest. Become my servants and learn from me. I am gentle and free of pride. You will find rest for your souls. Serving me is easy, and my load is light.
MATTHEW 11:28–30

Jesus did more than just die for our sins. He came to give us freedom, hope, joy, life. One of his most famous sayings is found in Matthew 11:28–30. There he tells the rule-weary people of his day that if they come to him, he will give them rest. Real rest. He assures them that serving him is easy, and any load he gives will be light.

Have you ever felt as if life is nothing but one rule after another? Would you like some rest from having to obey all the rules?

Jesus is the answer. He came to give us that rest. When we come to him and follow him, he enables us to obey the rules without even thinking about them. Without even fighting against them.

Have you trusted him for everything?

Trusting you about everything, Jesus, is hard. I so want to do my own thing. Help me to learn this truth in my life. Amen.

THEME: JESUS

Our Best Friend

You are my friends if you do what I command.

JOHN 15:14

Jesus isn't just God in human flesh, and the perfect man. He's something else: He is our friend.

Have you ever thought of Jesus as a friend? He said this in John 15:14: "You are my friends if you do what I command." What does a friend do? One of the things Jesus says earlier in the same passage is that a true friend will lay down his life for the one he loves.

That's what Jesus did: He gave his life for you, so you and I could live.

What does he ask in return? Obedience. Not to a set of rules. But to him, personally, freely.

Is Jesus your friend? Are you his friend? There's only one way to tell: Are you obeying him?

I pray, Lord, that I will obey you the way you want me to. Just show me the way to do it. In Jesus' name, amen.

"I Have Seen the Lord"

Mary Magdalene went to the disciples with the news. She said, "I have seen the Lord!" And she told them that he had said these things to her.

JOHN 20:18

How do we know for certain that Jesus rose from the dead? The New Testament gives us the facts:

1. Jesus predicted he would rise from the dead.
2. Jesus died on the cross. He was pierced in the side by a Roman spear. Water and blood came out, meaning he had been dead long enough for the blood and the serum to separate.
3. He was placed in a guarded tomb.
4. Many different people admitted something happened: the soldiers, the Pharisees, the disciples, and other observers.
5. Jesus appeared many times to his followers over the next forty days.

Jesus' resurrection is the most stupendous fact of history. Therefore, it's worth studying. Come along this week to learn more about the Resurrection.

I like facts, Father, and I like learning them. But help me to remember the Person behind the facts. In Jesus, amen.

THEME: THE RESURRECTION

He Told When and How

From that time on Jesus began to explain to his disciples what would happen to him. He told them he must go to Jerusalem. There he must suffer many things from the elders, the chief priests and the teachers of the law. He must be killed and on the third day rise to life again.

MATTHEW 16:21

Few people can predict the time, place, and circumstances of their death. Most of us simply don't know when God will call us out of this world.

But Jesus knew ahead of time that he would die and rise again the third day. He told his disciples this many times. In Matthew 16:21 he told the disciples he would go to Jerusalem and be delivered into the hands of the priests and elders. They would kill him and he would rise from the dead three days later.

Why did Jesus tell his disciples this? To prepare them, of course. But for another reason: so that they would know that it was all part of God's plan.

Your death is part of God's plan, too. And so is your resurrection. Have you put your faith in the One who can make you live forever?

Let me put my faith in the truth, Jesus, so I might give others the truth. In you, amen.

THEME: THE RESURRECTION

A Plot?

After Jesus cried out again in a loud voice, he died. At that moment the temple curtain was torn in two from top to bottom. The earth shook. The rocks split. Tombs broke open. The bodies of many holy people who had died were raised to life.
MATTHEW 27:50–52

Every few years some author comes out with a new theory of Jesus' resurrection. One famed book, "The Passover Plot," suggests that Jesus plotted to fake his death. Next, he would fake his resurrection. Is this possible?

Listen to what happened the minute Jesus died according to Matthew 27:50–52.

He cried out with a loud voice. He gave up his spirit. Darkness was on the land. The temple curtain ripped in two (to show that God had opened up the way for anyone to go into the holiest place). There was an earthquake. Rocks split. And some people rose again.

It's written like a newspaper story. "This happened. These are the facts."

It's up to us to believe them.

Father, thank you that Jesus rose again. Because of him, I know now I'll live forever with him. I praise you for that. In Jesus, amen.

THEME: THE RESURRECTION

The Guard at the Tomb

So they went and made the tomb secure. They put a seal on the stone and placed some guards on duty.

MATTHEW 27:66

After Jesus died on the cross, the leaders of the Jews wanted his tomb guarded. So they sealed the tomb and placed a Roman guard there. Why did they do this? Because they knew Jesus had predicted he'd rise from the dead. They believed the disciples would steal the body, and then the "last lie will be worse than the first" (Matthew 27:64).

What happened to that guard? Matthew 28:2–4 says, "There was a powerful earthquake. An angel of the Lord came down from heaven. The angel went to the tomb. He rolled back the stone and sat on it. His body shown like lightning. . . . The guards were so afraid of him that they shook and became like dead men."

It makes sense, doesn't it? Wouldn't the guards be terrified at such an event? Christian truth isn't based on stories; it's based on facts. It's based on evidence, the accounts of those who saw these things happen.

I'm so glad, Lord, that our faith is based on facts. Let me learn all the facts I can, so I will be confident of what I believe. Amen.

THEME: THE RESURRECTION

Death Is Conquered

On the evening of that first day of the week, the disciples were together. They had locked the doors because they were afraid of the Jews. Jesus came in and stood among them. He said, "May peace be with you!"

JOHN 20:19–20

Sunday night was an exciting night for the disciples. Reports were all over that Jesus had risen from the dead. He'd come to Peter personally. He'd spoken to two disciples as they traveled to a nearby town.

But now the stage is set. Will everyone see him at once? Yes. John 20:19 says the disciples had locked themselves in the room. Then Jesus came. He spoke to them and assured them of peace.

Apparently, Jesus passed right through the doors. But he wasn't a ghost. He would let the disciples touch him. At one point he would eat a fish.

But when he first appears, they're amazed. They can't believe this is happening. Who would? And Jesus greets them with the words, "Peace be with you!"

What a great greeting. Death is conquered. There's no reason to ever fear again. Jesus is alive, and he will take us to his home when he returns.

I praise you, God, that Jesus is with me. Amen.

THEME: THE RESURRECTION

He Appeared to Many

He appeared to Peter. Then he appeared to the Twelve. After that, he appeared to more than 500 believers at the same time. Most of them are still living. But some have died. He appeared to James. Then he appeared to all the apostles. Last of all, he also appeared to me.

1 CORINTHIANS 15:5–8

Who did Jesus appear to during the forty days following his resurrection? Paul gives us this list:

1. Peter
2. The Twelve
3. More than 500 people at once
4. James
5. All the missionary leaders
6. Paul himself

Notice: 500 people at once. That's a lot of eyewitnesses. This was no faked resurrection. If Jesus was faking it, how did he walk around in perfect health after being nailed to a cross? It's impossible.

Jesus conquered death so that no one who believes in him need fear death. Ever!

Father, sometimes I fear death. But thanks to you, I no longer have to because of Jesus' resurrection. Amen.

THEME: THE RESURRECTION

A Very Convincing Proof

Then he said to Thomas, "Put your finger here. See my hands. Reach out your hand and put it into my side. Stop doubting and believe." Thomas said to him, "My Lord and my God!"

JOHN 20:27–30

Thomas was the holdout. He wasn't there when Jesus first appeared to the disciples. And he didn't believe their stories. He wanted to find out for himself.

One night Jesus came into a room where all the disciples were. Jesus spoke to Thomas, inviting him to touch his hands and side. He said, "Stop doubting and believe." Thomas was so amazed, he fell to his knees and cried out, "My Lord and my God!"

Jesus didn't put down Thomas for doubting. Instead, he gave Thomas the chance to find out the truth the way he wanted to—by touching and seeing. If you have doubts, ask the Lord to confirm to you the truth.

That's the second way we know Jesus rose from the dead: God speaks to our own hearts about it. Has he spoken to you?

Speak to my heart, Jesus. Help me to know you are real. Amen.

THEME: THE RESURRECTION

God Will Never Desert us

God has said, "I will never leave you. I will never desert you."

HEBREWS 13:5

What is Jesus planning to do in our lives, in history, in the world?

Many things. But the first thing you need to know is that if you're a Christian, you will not be left out. I used to be so scared that Jesus would come back, but somehow he'd forget me. He'd be too busy, or maybe my name never got on his list. Maybe he just changed his mind about me.

You know what? That can never happen. Do you know what Jesus says about his commitment to us? He assures us he will never leave us or desert us. Never!

You don't ever need to fear that Jesus would desert you. If you believe in him, your name is in his book and he will stick by you forever. It's that sure.

Thank you, Jesus, for assuring me you will always be with me. I know that no matter what, with you there, I can face anything. Amen.

THEME: THE FUTURE

What Is Jesus Doing Now?

There are many rooms in my Father's house. If this were not true, I would have told you. I am going there to prepare a place for you. If I go and do that, I will come back. And I will take you to be with me. Then you will also be where I am.

JOHN 14:2–3

Do you know what Jesus is doing right now? He's preparing your house in heaven. Isn't that amazing? This is what he told his disciples in the verses you just read.

Right now Jesus is preparing the new place you will live in when you get to heaven. Can you imagine what that will be like? How many days did it take God to create the world? Six! But how many days has Jesus been up in heaven making his Father's house? Almost 2000 years. If God can create the whole world in six days, can you imagine what he can do in 2000 years?

I can't wait to see it. Can you?

I can't wait till the day comes, Father, when I enter my own house in heaven. Are you preparing one for my family, too? Amen.

THEME: THE FUTURE

The Great Catching Up

The Lord himself will come down from heaven. We will hear a loud command. We will hear the voice of the leader of the angels. We will hear a blast from God's trumpet. Many who believe in Christ will have died already. They will rise first. After that, we who are still alive and are left will be caught up together with them. We will be taken up in the clouds. We will meet the Lord in the air. And we will be with him forever.

1 THESSALONIANS 4:16–17

What's the next thing Jesus will do in human history? The event is called the second coming of Christ. It will be when he returns to gather those who belong to him.

This is what Paul tells us in 1 Thessalonians 4:16–17, the main passage about this event. There he tells us that God's trumpet will blast its sound all over the world. Everywhere, believers who have died will be wrenched from their graves and meet the Lord in the air. After that, believers who are still alive will also be snatched up into the air. That's you and me.

The Second Coming can happen at any moment. Are you ready for it?

Lord, may you come soon. Amen.

THEME: THE FUTURE

Every Eye Will See Him

I saw heaven standing open. There in front of me was a white horse. Its rider is called Faithful and True. When he judges or makes war, he is always fair.

REVELATION 19:11

What will happen at the end of time? Scholars disagree on what the exact sequence of events is, but the main one everyone agrees on is the second coming of Jesus. That's when he actually comes back to earth, stops all wars and sin, and begins to rule the world.

In Revelation 19:11, John tells us that heaven will suddenly open. Jesus will come on a white horse. Everyone will see him. And many will fear. He will end all wars and bring about perfect justice in the world.

But you never need to be afraid of his coming. Why? Because he's coming to set up a kingdom in which you and I will be rulers!

Could this be the day you come, Lord? Help me to be ready and not doing anything I'd be ashamed of when you come. In Jesus, amen.

THEME: THE FUTURE

No More Evil Anywhere!

I saw a new heaven and a new earth. The first heaven and the first earth were completely gone. There was no longer any sea.

REVELATION 21:1

Another event coming along in the future is God's new creation. He plans to start over. No more sin. No more hatred. No more racism. No more evil people doing evil things.

This is how John pictured it in Revelation 21:1: A new heaven and earth. The old heaven and earth gone. No sea anywhere to be seen.

God is going to make a new heaven and earth. He'll deal with all the pollution we've done. He'll fix all the lands and deserts. He'll make everything new.

Imagine what it would be like living in such a world. No bullies. No homework. No boring weekends. It'll be the greatest kingdom that has ever existed.

And you will be part of it!

There are so many in our world who don't know you, Lord. I pray for_____ that they will be ready when Jesus comes to start his kingdom. Amen.

THEME: THE FUTURE

God Will Be God of Everyone

I heard a loud voice from the throne. It said, "Now God makes his home with human beings. He will live with them. They will be his people. And God himself will be with them and be their God."

REVELATION 21:3

Do you know another wonderful thing Jesus plans for us in the future? God will be among us. We'll see his face. We'll run with him. We'll talk with him. He will be our greatest friend, and he will be available to each of us for whatever we need.

We don't know exactly how it will happen. How could the infinite God be in real space and time? We don't know. How could God talk to each of us at the same time? We don't know. How could he have the time for each of us, when there will probably be billions of us in that new world? No one knows.

But it's going to happen!

Some of the members of my family don't know you, Lord. Will you work in _____, _____, and _____. I want them to be in your new world. In Jesus, amen.

No More Death

He will wipe every tear from their eyes. There will be no more death or sadness. There will be no more crying or pain. Things are no longer the way they used to be.

REVELATION 21:4

Do you know the greatest thing about God's new world? There will be no more pain, death, or weeping for what we've lost. Can you imagine that?

John says there will be no more death or sadness. No more crying or pain. Everything will be new and different.

I remember when my grandfather died when I was fourteen years old. He was my greatest friend. He gave me my first jackknife. He taught me to split wood, skip stones, fish for bass, tell a joke, and love life. He had a stroke one night and was gone. At his funeral, all the family passed by the coffin for one last look. When that coffin was closed, I lost it. At the time I wasn't a Christian, and I had no hope of life after death.

But now I know that I'll see Grandpop again. Why? Because of what Jesus has done, and will do.

Lord, I look forward to the day I'll see my loved ones in heaven. In Jesus' name, amen.

THEME: THE FUTURE

God Wants Worshipers

But a new time is coming. In fact, it is already here. True worshipers will worship the Father in spirit and in truth. They are the kind of worshipers the Father is looking for.

JOHN 4:23

Did you know that God seeks worshipers? He does. He looks throughout the world constantly to find those people who truly want to exalt and love him. That's what Jesus told a Samaritan woman in John 4:23. A new time is coming when people will worship God in spirit and in truth. In fact, God seeks exactly that kind of worshiper.

Why do you think God seeks worshipers? Is it because he gets bored and has nothing better to do? Or is it because he thinks he's so great that he should have lots of people telling him he's great? Or is it because he doesn't like anyone else getting encouraged and built up?

None of the above! God seeks worshipers because he wants people to know what he's really like. And only through worship can that happen.

So find out all about God. Worship him today!

Eternal God, you are so great! Thank you for showing me more of your greatness every day. Amen.

THEME: WORSHIP

In Spirit and in Truth

God is spirit. His worshipers must worship him in spirit and in truth.

JOHN 4:24

How are we to worship God? Here, Jesus says we are to worship God on two levels: in spirit and in truth. What does that mean?

Our spirit is the deepest, most intimate, and personal part of us. It is who and what we are in our deepest thoughts and feelings. To worship God "in spirit" means we worship him with our most personal part. We hold back nothing. Our whole being is caught up in praising and loving him.

To worship "in truth" means that there's no pretense, no lying, no faking it. What you see on the outside is what's going on inside. We really do love him and worship him in our deepest being.

Have you ever worshiped God like that? Would you like to?

Teach me to worship in spirit and truth, Lord, like you say. I want to do that with all my heart. Amen.

THEME: WORSHIP

The Eyes of God

The LORD looks out over the whole earth. He gives strength to those who commit their lives completely to him.
2 CHRONICLES 16:9

Right now God is on the lookout. Did you know that? Oh, he's not looking to find fault or to complain about us. No, he wants to support people who love and worship him. Imagine if you had God supporting you in everything. What would happen in your life?

This is what it says in 2 Chronicles 16:9: "The LORD looks out over the whole earth. He gives strength to those who commit their lives completely to him."

God is watching right now. He looks at your heart—your spirit—and he asks, "Is this person completely on my side? Does he or she thoroughly support my plan and my kingdom?"

When the answer comes up "YES!" you win the prize! What prize? The prize of God's complete and unswerving help. For everything.

If you respond to him like that, you can never fail!

I want Jesus' complete support. Help me to let him work in my life. In his name, amen.

THEME: WORSHIP

God Looks at the Heart

Do not consider how handsome or tall he is. I have not chosen him. I do not look at the things people look at. They look at how someone appears on the outside. But I look at what is in the heart.

1 SAMUEL 16:7

When God needed a ruler to replace the wicked King Saul, he sent his prophet Samuel to a family that lived near Bethlehem. This family had many sons. When Samuel came to them, he was very impressed. But as he stepped up to each son, God told him, "No, this isn't the one." Samuel didn't know what to think.

Then they brought in the last son: David. This boy would ultimately become Israel's greatest king. Why? God told Samuel not to look at the outward appearance. Is someone handsome? That's not enough. Is he well built? No, still not enough. Is he a warrior, able to fight? Good, but not enough.

No, God looks at the heart—who you are on the inside. He looks for people who worship him with their whole hearts. What do you think God sees when he looks at your heart?

I know sometimes, Lord, that my heart isn't in my worship of you. Give me an obedient heart like David's. Amen.

THEME: WORSHIP

Lip Service

These people worship me only with their words. They honor me by what they say. But their hearts are far away from me. Their worship doesn't mean anything to me. They teach nothing but human rules.

ISAIAH 29:13

What do you see when you go to church? Does everyone pay attention? Or do they act bored? Do they speak prayers with gusto, or do they recite words without thinking?

One of God's biggest complaints about humanity is that they fake worship all the time. In fact, this is how Isaiah, one of Israel's greatest prophets, said it in the passage above: They have lots of words. They speak well. They craft great rules. But one thing is missing: their hearts.

Following the rules is wise. But it can be wooden, forced, halfhearted.

God wants "heart" worship, the kind of worship that comes from the deepest part of us. Is that the way you're worshiping God these days? If not, tell him you're sorry, and ask him to give you some help!

Let our church, Jesus, worship you with all our heart, soul, mind, and might. Amen.

THEME: WORSHIP

Our God Is Awesome

We are receiving a kingdom that can't be shaken. So let us be thankful. Then we can worship God in a way that pleases him. We will worship him with deep respect and wonder.

HEBREWS 12:28

Ginny asked her teacher, "What's the main thing in worship? What does God want from me?"

Her teacher thought, and finally said, "I guess it would be awe."

Awe. What's that? You've probably used the word *awesome*. Something is awesome when it's amazing, great, incredible, wonderful, and almost too good to be true.

That's what God also wants from us in worship. Awe. He wants us to be a bit amazed, astonished at who he is and what he is like. The passage from Hebrews says it well. We are to worship with "respect and wonder." That's reverence and awe!

Awe is not so hard, though. When you read the Bible and find out what God has done and can do, aren't you amazed at times?

Sometimes I don't feel much awe, Lord. It seems all the same to me. Open my eyes that I might see you with awe. Amen.

THEME: WORSHIP

What God Most Wants from You

Brothers and sisters, God has shown you his mercy. So I am asking you to offer up your bodies to him while you are still alive. Your bodies are a holy sacrifice that is pleasing to God. When you offer your bodies to God, you are worshiping him.

ROMANS 12:1

If there's one thing you could do that God most wants from you, what would it be? Give all your money to his work? Serve him in the church as a teacher, pastor, or leader? Lead a hundred kids to him? Go to a foreign land and tell people there about Jesus?

None of the above!

No, Paul told the Romans in the verse above that what God wants is your body. That means God wants you to present your body—all of yourself—to him as a spiritual sacrifice. He will then use you to do some and maybe all of those other things.

All God is saying is this: Give me yourself, and I'll give you everything else!

Right now, Father, I present my body to you. Use me as you see fit all the rest of the days of my life. Amen.

THEME: WORSHIP

Bad Company

Don't let anyone fool you. "Bad companions make a good person bad."

1 CORINTHIANS 15:33

Jeremy picked up the phone and dialed the number. Ken answered. "Ken, I've got to show you something," Jeremy said. "It's the greatest."

"What?" Ken asked.

Jeremy told him, and Ken gasped. "Jeremy, you shouldn't ..."

"Oh, don't give me a lecture. It's cool. Come on over, and I'll show you."

Ken and Jeremy are friends, but for Ken it might not be a wise friendship. Why? Because Jeremy is into things that are wrong.

Paul said, "Bad companions make good people bad." When you hang out with the wrong kind of people, you're in danger. Your good life can easily be made bad.

Take a look at your friends. Who are they? What are they into? Is it wise for you to stick with them?

My friend, _____, Lord, sometimes tempts me to do wrong things. Help me to stand up to him and do what's right. Amen.

THEME: FRIENDS

The True Friend

Even those who have many companions can be destroyed. But there is a friend who sticks closer than a brother.

PROVERBS 18:24

Who should you pick as a friend? Solomon pointed out that having a lot of friends doesn't necessarily make you invincible. Instead, one good friend will stick closer than a brother. That's the right friend to choose.

Having lots of friends is fine. But much better is a friend who sticks closer than a brother. What does that mean? Friends who spend time with you, know you, and are loyal to you are friends worth having. How do you know if a friend is loyal? Here are three tests:

1. Does he/she listen to you and try to understand your feelings and ideas?
2. Does he/she offer help when you need it?
3. Does he/she point out to you when you're making a mistake?

When you find a true friend, stick close!

I want real friends, Father, the type who will speak the truth to me. Show me such people and help me befriend them. Amen.

THEME: FRIENDS

A Friend Loves All the Time

Friends love at all times. They are there to help when trouble comes.

PROVERBS 17:17

What does a friend do? He "loves at all times," according to Solomon.

Solomon would know. His father, King David, had a friend—Jonathan—who became the best friend David ever had. Jonathan defended David to his father, King Saul, who wanted to kill David. Jonathan helped David escape death several times. He spent time with David, sharing his life with the young man. And Jonathan ultimately laid his life on the line for David.

A friend never ceases to love. Oh, you may have a fight. You may disagree about something. You may even go separate ways for a time. But a true friend will always renew ties.

Look for a friend like that, and when you have found him, don't let him go.

_____ is a good friend, Master. Work in her and make our friendship beautiful in your eyes. In Jesus' name, amen.

THEME: FRIENDS

The Tricks of Friendship

Then Hushai, the Arkite, went to Absalom. He said to him, "May the king live a long time!" ... Hushai was David's friend. Absalom asked Hushai, "Is this the way you show love to your friend? Why didn't you go with him?" Hushai said to Absalom, "Why should I? You are the one the LORD has chosen. These people and all the men of Israel have also chosen you. I want to be on your side."

2 SAMUEL 16:16–17

King David had a problem. His son Absalom had rebelled and taken many men with him. Now David needed to do some spying. But who could he rely on?

He had a ready answer: his friend Hushai. In 2 Samuel 16:16–17, we read that Hushai pretended to be Absalom's friend in order to get information about his plans to David. Hushai risked his life to spy for his friend David! In the end, he provided invaluable help. Absalom should have been very wary. He knew Hushai was a good friend of David's. A good friend will risk anything for the one he loves.

Is that the kind of friend you are to your friends?

Let me be the kind of friend who is loyal, Lord. Sometimes I gossip and talk about my friends, and I know I shouldn't. In Jesus, amen.

THEME: FRIENDS

A Friend Indeed

But Ruth replied, "Don't try to make me leave you and go back. Where you go I'll go. Where you stay I'll stay. Your people will be my people. Your God will be my God."

RUTH 1:16

Hanging his head, the young man stood before the judge in the courtroom. A sentence was about to be announced. But suddenly, another young man stepped up to the railing. "Judge," he said, "can I say something?"

The judge motioned for him to speak. At that point, the young man launched into a speech about why his friend, the defendant, should be given a lighter sentence. "He's a good kid," he said. "He helped me build my tree fort. He rescued me once when I was almost drowning. And he encouraged me to return something I'd stolen. I promise, sir, if you let him go, I'll stick by him and make sure he doesn't do this crime again."

The judge was amazed. And he decided not to pronounce a stiff sentence.

There is no friend like one who will plead your case for you. If you find a friend like that, hold him tight.

My friends are so important to me, Father. Help me encourage and love them the way Jesus does. Amen.

THEME: FRIENDS

The Danger of Rumors

Those who erase a sin by forgiving it show love. But those who talk about it come between close friends.

PROVERBS 17:9

"Did you hear what Jane said about you?" Sarah asked at the lunch table.

Liz leaned close to hear.

Sarah told the whole story, and Liz was angry. When Jane walked in and sat down with them, a cool silence fell. Jane stared at them. "What's the matter?" she finally said.

Liz glared at her. "I heard what you said about me!"

Nothing messes up a friendship like repeating things that should be forgotten. It can be gossip, a lie, a rumor, or anything like that. But it can ruin a friendship. As Solomon pointed out, repeating a sin to another person makes it worse and separates close friends.

If a friend says or does something you know is wrong, don't tell others about it. Tell the friend and encourage him to stop saying or doing such things. That's the way to keep a friend and right a wrong.

Help me not to gossip about others, Master. I know I shouldn't and I'm ashamed when I do. Amen.

THEME: FRIENDS

Telling the Truth

Wounds from a friend can be trusted. But an enemy kisses you many times.

PROVERBS 27:6

"Les, I have something to say to you," Jill said, "and I know you won't like it."

"What?"

"Do you know what you sound like when you swear?"

"I don't swear that much."

"You swear a lot. And it hurts people."

"Who?"

At that point, Jill began the hard work of telling Les about some kids he had hurt with his bad language.

Often the Holy Spirit will lead you to gently tell the truth about some problem to someone else. When God wounds a friend with the truth like that, real healing will follow. But an enemy just kisses you. And then stabs you in the back.

When God's Spirit tells you the truth through a friend, listen, even when it hurts.

_____ *said something to me I didn't like, Father, because it was true. Help me to listen when my friends speak the truth. In Jesus, amen.*

Fruit the Spirit Produces in us

But the fruit the Holy Spirit produces is love, joy and peace. It is being patient, kind and good. It is being faithful and gentle and having control of oneself. There is no law against things of that kind.

GALATIANS 5:22–23

Many people do not understand the Spirit of God. They imagine him to be a "force" like in the Star Wars movies, or a "thing," like a ghost of some sort. The truth is he is a person. God exists as three persons—the Father, Son, and Spirit. All are divine. They are separate personalities, but they are linked together by one reality: God himself.

It's probably easier, though, to think of the Spirit in terms of what he does. And one of the primary things he does is produce fruit in a believer's life. What is that fruit? Paul lists the characteristics in Galatians 5:22–23: love, joy, peace, patience, kindness, goodness, faithfulness, gentleness, and self-control.

The Spirit wants to produce all these qualities in your life, every day, in every situation. Will you let him do that?

Lord, produce all your fruit in my life and especially today. In Jesus, amen.

THEME: THE HOLY SPIRIT

Love Poured Out on Us

God has poured his love into our hearts. He did it through the Holy Spirit, whom he has given to us.

ROMANS 5:5

Becky sat in her seat, crying. "But how do I know God loves me?"

"Jesus died for you," the teacher said.

"But that's so far away. I need something close."

"Like a hug?"

"Sort of."

"Well, that's exactly how the Spirit loves us. Let me show you." The teacher opened her Bible to Romans 5:5 and read how God poured his love into our hearts through the Holy Spirit.

What does this mean? God puts the Spirit into our hearts, and the Spirit speaks to us in that still, small voice. He tells us, "I love you. I care about you. I will never leave you."

Start listening. If you're a Christian, he's there and he speaks.

Open my ears and my eyes, Lord, that I might hear you speak and lead. Amen.

THEME: THE HOLY SPIRIT

Your Body: A Temple

Don't you know that your bodies are temples of the Holy Spirit? The Spirit is in you. You have received him from God. You do not belong to yourselves. Christ has paid the price for you. So use your bodies in a way that honors God.

1 CORINTHIANS 6:19–20

"It's my body," James said as he lit a cigarette. "I can do what I want with it."

James's father shook his head. "You're twelve years old. That's too young to smoke!"

"It's my life."

"No, it's not!"

James peered at his dad. "What do you mean?"

"Look at what Paul says in 1 Corinthians 6:19. Your body is a temple where the Holy Spirit lives. Do you want to junk up God's temple with smoke, dirt, and filth? No way. You aren't your own, James. You belong to God. And if you belong to him, act like it."

With that, his father took the cigarette out of his hand and snuffed it out.

Loving Father, may I always treat my body as your temple. Amen.

THEME: THE HOLY SPIRIT

What the Kingdom of God Is Like

God's kingdom has nothing to do with eating or drinking. It is a matter of being right with God. It brings the peace and joy the Holy Spirit gives.

ROMANS 14:17

What is the Holy Spirit trying to bring into our lives? Besides his fruit, Romans 14:17 says there are three things he's working to produce: righteousness, peace, and joy. Let's look at these realities.

Righteousness—that's right living, doing the right thing, being honest and truthful.

Peace—that's the relational side of the Spirit's work. He's trying to help us get along with everyone. No fights. No hatred. No prejudice.

Joy—that's the personal side of it. Holy, healthy, face-splitting joy! Feeling good and free and alive and happy.

Ask God to begin putting those things into your life today. You'll never look back.

Bring peace and joy into my life daily, Lord. Amen.

THEME: THE HOLY SPIRIT

Making the Holy Spirit Sad

Do not make God's Holy Spirit sad. He marked you with a seal for the day when God will set you completely free.

EPHESIANS 4:30

Did you know you can make the Holy Spirit weep?

Yes, you can. It says so in Ephesians 4:30: "Do not make God's Holy Spirit sad."

To "grieve" the Spirit or make him sad means to put him to grief, to make him cry, to hurt his heart. How does one do that? Through sin. But not just mistake-sins. No, we especially grieve him when we know something is wrong, but we don't care and we do it anyway.

Like the time Jesse lied to his mom about doing his homework on time.

Like when Amelia wrote in ink on her brother's baseball mitt because she was mad at him.

Like when . . . Put in your own experience. When we do what's wrong, knowing it's wrong, we grieve God's Spirit.

I know the Spirit has probably wept over me sometimes, Lord. Help me to please him in all that I do. In Jesus' name, amen.

THEME: THE HOLY SPIRIT

The Challenge of Serving God

We and the Lord were your examples. You followed us. You suffered terribly. Even so, you welcomed our message with the joy the Holy Spirit gives.

1 THESSALONIANS 1:6

"They hate me," Tyler said to his dad, sniffling. "Everyone at school hates me because I told them Jesus was the Savior of the world and the only way to heaven."

"Everyone?" asked Tyler's dad.

"They all do, Dad," Tyler said. "Only Stevie Rice and Jimmy Doolins acted okay."

"You know what God says when people hate us because we've done something good?"

"What?"

"He gives us joy in the Holy Spirit."

God does. When we suffer for the name of Jesus, it's like a badge of courage. God rewards us with joy, if we'll just look for it. Like 1 Thessalonians 1:6 says, God gives us joy when we hear the Good News. Even when we suffer for it. Why? Because the Good News is such good news!

Sometimes I think that _____ hates me because I love you, Lord. Help me to love him like you do. Amen.

THEME: THE HOLY SPIRIT

Becoming Born Again

He saved us. It wasn't because of the good things we had done. It was because of his mercy. He saved us by washing away our sins. We were born again. The Holy Spirit gave us new life.

TITUS 3:5

How does a person become born again? By believing in Jesus, right? But what happens on God's side?

Scripture says that the Spirit works in our hearts to open our minds and show us the truth. This is what it says in Titus 3:5: God gave us new life by having the Holy Spirit open our eyes and help us believe.

The Spirit of God works both rebirth and renewal into our lives. How does he do that?

1. He draws us to Jesus. He gets us interested (John 6:44).
2. He opens our hearts to the truth so that we listen (Acts 16:14).
3. He shows us how to pray (Romans 8:26–27).

Have you allowed the Spirit to do those works in your life?

Work in my life, Spirit of God, and make me like Jesus. Amen.

THEME: THE HOLY SPIRIT

Learning to Walk

I am the light of the world. Those who follow me will never walk in darkness. They will have the light that leads to life.
JOHN 8:12

The one-year-old shakily stood. His legs wobbled. He staggered. Then he tumbled to the floor, screaming.

Day by day his parents worked with him. Soon, he could stand without falling. He was shaky, but learning.

Next, he took his first steps.

After that, it was real walking, then running.

That's your story. Every one of us learned to walk that way.

In the spiritual realm, it works the same way. When we first become Christians, we're like babies. We can't walk, and we can hardly feed ourselves. But soon we take those first steps. Eventually, we learn to walk in Jesus' light. As we do that, we see the road ahead and do not fear what's around the corner.

Let me walk in the light, Father, that I might see all that I do both right and wrong. That way I know I'll please you. Amen.

THEME: WALKING WITH JESUS

Walk and Be Blameless

When Abram was 99 years old, the LORD appeared to him. He said, "I am the Mighty God. Walk with me and live without any blame."

GENESIS 17:1

Walking with Jesus is not difficult. We learn to listen to him through the Bible. We speak to him in prayer. And the Spirit of God goes with us in the daily circumstances of life. He whispers guidance to us, and helps us see the way.

It was a little like what happened to Abraham. In Genesis 17:1, God appeared to Abram (this was before God changed his name to Abraham) and told him, "Walk with me and live without any blame."

What did God mean by "walk with me and live without any blame"? He meant, "Live out your life in a good, righteous way. Do what's right in every situation of life. Live as if I'm right there beside you, because I am!"

God is with you. Jesus is with you. The Spirit is with you. How can you fail to succeed?

Thank you, perfect Master, that you are with me. I know I don't have to be afraid of anyone or anything. In Jesus' name, amen.

THEME: WALKING WITH JESUS

God Has Prepared the Way

God made us. He created us to belong to Christ Jesus. Now we can do good things. Long ago God prepared them for us to do.

EPHESIANS 2:10

Do you see something marvelous God has done? Each day he has prepared experiences for you to go through. And how you deal with those situations will reveal to the world you belong to him.

Did you know that? God has a fight planned here that you can break up. He has some dishes to wash at home that will help your mom. He has a paper you can help your sister write. And many other things.

Look at what Paul wrote in Ephesians 2:10: God wants us to do "good things." Because he prepared them for us to do "long ago."

Walking with Jesus is living for him every moment. It's doing what he says is right every step of the way.

Can you imagine what an adventure God has planned for you today?

Lord, what good deeds have you planned for me today? Help me do what pleases you when I find them. Amen.

THEME: WALKING WITH JESUS

Walking in the Light

But suppose we walk in the light, just as he is in the light. Then we share life with one another. And the blood of Jesus, his Son, makes us pure from all sin.

1 JOHN 1:7

Abigail stood at the front door in the dark, fumbling with her keys. "Why didn't Mom leave the light on?" she grumbled.

Suddenly, behind her she heard a growl.

Whipping around, she searched the darkness. Another growl. Something was out there, and she didn't know what it was.

Have you ever had that experience? Darkness can be scary—and dangerous.

Do you know what's worse? Spiritual darkness. When you don't know what's right or wrong, when you're not sure if there's a heaven or hell, when you don't have a heavenly Father who loves you.

God doesn't want us to live in the dark. When we know God, we walk in his light. In the light, we have security, hope, safety. That's how God wants us to live!

Help me to walk in your light, dear God. Protect me from the forces of darkness. Amen.

THEME: WALKING WITH JESUS

How Does God Want us to Live?

The way we show our love is to obey God's commands. He commands you to lead a life of love. That's what you have heard from the beginning.

2 JOHN 6

What is the main way God wants us to live?

The answer is found in 2 John 1:6. There, John says, "He commands you to lead a life of love."

How do you lead a life of love?

- By offering to help Mom or Dad when they need it.
- By comforting a little child when he's crying.
- By telling others about Jesus and his love.
- By being honest and telling the truth.
- By writing thank-you notes to relatives after Christmas.
- By letting a friend ride your bike or use your roller blades.

There are a million ways to do it. Just ask, "How would I want others to treat me?" Then go and treat them that way!

Let me obey the Golden Rule, Jesus, so that I might treat others the way I want to be treated. Amen.

THEME: WALKING WITH JESUS

Walk in the Truth

Some believers came to me and told me that you are faithful to the truth. They told me that you continue to live by it. That gave me great joy.

3 John 1:3

There's another part of walking with Jesus that John speaks of. It's walking in truth. John says in 3 John 1:3 above that the believers he was writing to were "faithful to the truth." They "lived by it." That gave John great joy.

God wants us to walk in the truth. But what does that mean? Here are several ways:

- Admitting you're wrong when you are.
- Confessing your sins to God each day.
- Telling God thanks when he has blessed you.
- Speaking the truth to a friend who has done something wrong.

Walking in truth isn't hard. Just do what God's Word says and that's it, because God's Word *is* the truth!

Show me something new today, Father, that I might obey. I want to please you every moment of the day. In Jesus, amen.

THEME: WALKING WITH JESUS

How Will We Live in Heaven?

But you have a few people in Sardis who have kept their clothes clean. They will walk with me, dressed in white, because they are worthy.

REVELATION 3:4

"When I get to heaven, I'm going to have a great bike, and all the Nintendo games ever invented," Sam said.

Jordan replied, "I can't wait to get to the ice-cream store in heaven. I bet they have a million and two flavors."

Beth added, "I'm gonna have a great dollhouse. All the best pieces of furniture, and a canopy bed."

Heaven will be a great experience. Maybe there will even be bikes and Nintendo, ice cream and canopy beds there. But do you know what will be the best part of heaven?

Jesus told the church of Sardis in Revelation 3:4 what that will be: We will walk with Jesus in white.

The greatest thing about heaven will be walking with Jesus. Side by side. Right up the road.

Forever.

Lord, I'm excited about the day when we'll be with you forever. Let me be faithful till that day comes. Amen.

THEME: WALKING WITH JESUS

Satan, the Enemy of God's People

Control yourselves. Be on your guard. Your enemy the devil is like a roaring lion. He prowls around looking for someone to chew up and swallow.

1 PETER 5:8

Who is Satan?

His name means "adversary" or "opponent." According to Ezekiel 28:11–19, Satan had the top position in God's angelic creation. He was a "coverer," meaning that he protected the glory of God against any attack. He had privileges galore and wore a robe of jewels. He was beautiful, powerful, and highly intelligent.

But something went wrong. He became proud and jealous of God's position. He wanted to be worshiped like God was. So he began a rebellion that ultimately led one-third of the angels of heaven against God.

Now Satan roams the earth with his demonic horde looking for anyone on God's side. Peter warns us that we should be on guard, because Satan wants to devour all who stand for God.

He's looking for you. Fortunately, you're under God's protection!

Give me courage, Father, so that when Satan comes by I'll be ready. In Jesus' name, amen.

THEME: THE ENEMY

When Satan Appeared Before God

One day angels came to the LORD. Satan also came with them.

JOB 1:6

One of the most interesting situations you'll find in the Bible is in Job 1. There, it says that when angels came before God, Satan was there with them (Job 1:6). Read the passage and you'll see something amazing: Satan challenged God to a duel. Not to a gunfight or sword fight, but to a truth fight. God asked Satan if the devil had noticed his faithful servant, Job. Satan had, and added that Job was "faithful" for only one reason: because God gave Job everything he wanted.

So what did God do? He told Satan he would take everything away from Job except his life. This was to see if Job would curse God.

The duel was on. Ultimately, God was proved right. Job didn't curse God.

That's the kind of enemy Satan is. He's always trying to prove that he is smarter than God. And he tries to use us to do it!

Protect me, Master, from the devil. I know his power, but I know you're more powerful than he is. Amen.

THEME: THE ENEMY

Stealing the Word Out of Their Mouths

What is seed scattered on a path like? The message is planted. The people hear the message. Then Satan comes. He takes away the message that was planted in them.

MARK 4:15

One of Satan's best tactics is to steal the truth from people. Jesus told a parable about it, called the Parable of the Sower. In it Jesus talks about a farmer strewing seed on the ground, much like a Christian tells his friends about Jesus. In some cases, listeners are like seed on a path. The ground is hard, so the seed doesn't lay down roots. In the light of the sun, birds come (Satan) and eat the seed. Then the seed is gone forever.

Right now, Satan and his demons are doing their best to keep God's Word from getting out. When some people hear the truth, Satan gets them to ignore it, hate it, reject it, spit on it, and forget it.

He's very successful, too. Look at how many people don't believe in Jesus.

The question is: Has Satan taken away the truth from you, too?

Don't let the devil take the truth from me, Lord, so I may walk in truth all the time. In Jesus, amen.

THEME: THE ENEMY

The Accuser

Then the LORD showed me the high priest Jeshua. He was standing in front of the angel of the LORD. Satan was standing to the right of Jeshua. He was there to bring charges against the high priest.

ZECHARIAH 3:1

This conversation might be happening in heaven right now: "God, did you see Mary today?"

"Yes."

"You heard her lie to her teacher about her homework?"

"Yes."

"Then how can you call her a Christian? She's a hypocrite! You should cast her into hell!"

What's happening here? A demon is accusing a Christian before God. That's one of the jobs of a devil—to accuse. When Jeshua the high priest appeared before God, Satan was right there with him. Satan's purpose: to bring charges against the high priest.

Satan accuses us constantly before God. But do you know what Jesus does, if we're Christians? He says, "That sin was paid for at the cross, Father. Away, Satan!"

Help me to please you, eternal Father, in everything I do, so Satan won't have anything to accuse me of. Amen.

THEME: THE ENEMY

Satan, the Master Tempter

The Holy Spirit led Jesus into the desert. There the devil tempted him.

MATTHEW 4:1

Besides accusing us, Satan also tempts us. Think of the last time you wanted to do something wrong. Did you hear words like this in your mind?

"Go ahead. No one will know."

Or, "You have a right to do that. Don't let people take advantage of you."

Or, "It'll make you feel good. Everyone should be allowed to feel good, shouldn't they?"

That's Satan talking! Whenever that little voice in your head tells you to do something you know is wrong, you can be sure Satan is tempting you.

But you know what? Jesus knows what it's like. He was tempted, too. And for that reason he can help us when we're tempted.

Strengthen my heart and mind, Master, to know when the devil is tempting me. Overcome him in me, I pray. Amen.

THEME: THE ENEMY

The Ultimate Test

Simon, Simon! Satan has asked to sift you disciples like wheat!

LUKE 22:31

"Just let me at him, and I'll show you what he's really like!" Ever hear someone say something like that? Such people think you have some flaw that they can expose.

Satan wanted to test Peter to find his flaws. Jesus revealed that Peter would fall to Satan's test, but that he shouldn't lose heart, because this test would be used to strengthen his fellow disciples.

Satan wanted to test Peter so severely he'd give up the faith. Satan wants to do the same thing to you. But he can't just do that. He has to ask God's permission first!

God is protecting you right now from the wiles and work of Satan. But every now and then he lets Satan have his way with one of us. And it's then that God shows himself even greater and more powerful than Satan.

I thank you for your protection, Jesus, and I ask you to watch over me and keep me from the devil's temptations. In your name, amen.

THEME: THE ENEMY

Jesus Has Overcome Satan

He grabbed the dragon, that old serpent. The serpent is also called the devil, or Satan. The angel put him in chains for 1,000 years.

REVELATION 20:2

All this talk about Satan may scare you. I hope not. Remember these three truths:

1. Satan can't tempt you or "sift" you unless God lets him (Luke 22:31–34).
2. Jesus defeated Satan at the cross and broke his power. Jesus is always greater than Satan (1 John 4:4).
3. God has given us all the tools we need to defeat Satan every time (Ephesians 6:11–18).

In the end, Satan will finally be defeated. Revelation 20:2 says, "He grabbed the dragon, that old serpent. The serpent is also called the devil, or Satan. The angel put him in chains for 1,000 years."

At the end of time, Satan will be bound and ultimately silenced. So don't worry about him too much. Rely on Jesus, and you will overcome.

Get my eyes on you, Father, and off of sin and the devil. With you, I know, I can succeed and win. Amen.

THEME: THE ENEMY

Standing Firm

Put on all of God's armor. Then you can stand firm against the devil's evil plans.

EPHESIANS 6:11

Every day, demons roam the earth, looking for unsuspecting Christians to attack. How do we defeat them? Paul told us to put on the armor of God, including these things:

> Belt of truth—God's truth as well as being truthful
>
> Armor of godliness—Christ's perfection as well as our own right behavior
>
> Good news of peace—readiness to share the gospel
>
> Shield of faith—personal faith in Christ
>
> Helmet of salvation—the knowledge that Jesus is your Savior
>
> Sword of the Spirit—God's Word
>
> Praying in the Spirit

With these weapons, you can defeat any demon, anytime, anywhere.

Dress me in your armor, Lord, and help me fight the devil with your weapons. Amen.

THEME: SPIRITUAL WARFARE

The Angels of Light

Even Satan himself pretends to be an angel of light.
2 CORINTHIANS 11:14

One of a demon's best tricks is to make you think he's on your side and wants you to do the right thing. For instance . . .

- He'll tell you to steal something in order to give it to your brother for a birthday present.
- He'll suggest that you cheat on a test to get a good grade so your dad will be pleased.
- He'll advise you that little "white lie" was to protect a friend.

Any devil has numerous tricks up his sleeve. But this is one of his best. Paul told us about this trick in 2 Corinthians 11:14: "Satan himself pretends to be an angel of light."

The enemy's best trick is to take the truth and twist it just a little. Watch out for it.

Help me to be on the alert, Father of truth, so Satan can't deceive me with his lies. Amen.

THEME: SPIRITUAL WARFARE

Don't Sin When You're Angry

When you are angry, do not sin.

EPHESIANS 4:26

"GET OUT OF MY ROOM OR I'LL BEAT YOU TO A PULP!"

"Okay, don't be so angry about it! I'm sorry."

"I HAVE A RIGHT TO BE ANGRY!"

Ever had that conversation with a brother or sister? Rooms are private. And little brothers and sisters are always sneaking into them. But do you have a right to be angry?

Do you know what the Bible says? Yes, you do have a right to be angry. Look at Ephesians 4:26: "When you are angry, do not sin." You can be angry, just don't be angry in a sinful way. Righteous anger doesn't use bad language, doesn't get violent, doesn't speak cruelly or nastily, doesn't boil over into hatred. When it does, this is giving the devil a foothold.

When we keep fuming and steaming, we give the devil a chance to plant seeds of hatred.

Sinful anger is one of the devil's best strategies to undo us.

Sometimes I get angry, Jesus. Work in my heart that I might be angry but not sin. Amen.

THEME: SPIRITUAL WARFARE

Weeds in the Wheat

A man planted good seed in his field. But while everyone was sleeping, his enemy came. The enemy planted weeds among the wheat and then went away.

MATTHEW 13:24–25

How do you wreck a church?

The devil is a master at it. Do you know what he does? He plants fakes in the church who stir it up with gossip, lying, rumors, ugly words, and the like. Jesus told his disciples in the Parable of the Weeds that the devil plants fake Christians in the church to bring it to ruin.

How can you tell a fake Christian?

By his fruit. What is his life producing? Good things—patience, kindness, truth—or bad things—violence, anger, nasty words? When you see a fellow Christian do those things, you should tell him to change his ways or change his church!

It's up to you. Stop the devil when you see him working. He won't return quickly to the same spot.

Some of my friends at church do wrong things, Lord. Work in them and change them, I pray, so you won't be dishonored. In Jesus' name, amen.

THEME: SPIRITUAL WARFARE

Demons Are Overcome by Jesus' Power

Dear children, you belong to God. You have not accepted the teachings of the false prophets. That's because the One who is in you is more powerful than the one who is in the world.

1 JOHN 4:4

Are we at the mercy of demons?

Some Christians would have us believe demons are everywhere. They're looking for every chance to hurt us. And many times they succeed.

The truth is that demons are at your mercy. All a demon can do is try to tempt you, trick you, or lie to you. He can't touch you unless God lets him, and God very rarely does that.

No, John gave us a powerful truth when he said in the passage above that Jesus is greater than the one who runs the world.

God is greater than Satan and all his demons. Don't be afraid to do what's right, even when threatened. God will be with you all the way.

Lord, I know you're greater than Satan, but sometimes he seems very powerful. Show me how to defeat him your way, I pray. Amen.

THEME: SPIRITUAL WARFARE

Demon Possession

When evening came, many people controlled by demons were brought to Jesus. He drove out the spirits with a word. He healed all who were sick.

MATTHEW 8:16

One of Scripture's strangest features is the many cases of demon possession. Scripture tells us that Jesus cast out many demons during his life on earth.

Could you ever become demon-possessed?

If you're a Christian, most people believe it's impossible. But who knows what could happen if you dabble in such things as . . .

Witchery
Ouija boards
Tarot cards
Mediums and fortune-telling
Satanism

Stay away from these things. They're dangerous, and if they hook you, they could harm you badly.

Father, I know Satan will do anything to destroy my friends and me. Protect us from ever doing anything that shames you. In Jesus' name, amen.

THEME: SPIRITUAL WARFARE

Evil Terminated

Then he will say to those on his left, "You are cursed! Go away from me into the fire that burns forever. It has been prepared for the devil and his angels."

Matthew 25:41

Will demons always be there to tempt us?

No, God promises that he will deal with every evil person, demon, angel, sinner, liar, and murderer. They will be stopped in their tracks. Matthew 25:41 tells of a judgment in which Jesus will send some people to hell. He says to them to depart from him and go into the eternal fire. It was prepared for the devil and his angels, but evil people will go there too.

God has prepared "eternal fire" for the devil and his angels. Their deeds will be exposed. Their power will be ended. And they will be confined forever in eternal fire.

You can be sure that if God has this planned for the end of time, he can help you now in the present. Seek his help through prayer and his Word, and you'll get to see the devil run.

I like winning over temptation, Lord. So help me today and always. In Jesus, amen.

THEME: SPIRITUAL WARFARE

Jesus Took Away All Our Sins

Look! The Lamb of God! He takes away the sin of the world!
JOHN 1:29

Doug looked down at the mower. He sure didn't want to cut the lawn. So he took off the top air cleaner and exposed the engine. Then he twisted several screws. That would fix it but good. He gave the starter cord a pull. The engine sputtered and died.

"Dad! Dad! The lawnmower won't work!"

Dad came out and looked at it. He began working with the screws. "Pull the starter cord while I get these adjusted," he said.

Doug pulled the starter cord. And pulled. And pulled. And pulled. By the time the engine started, he was exhausted.

"Just needed a little adjusting," Dad said. "Now go mow that lawn!"

Doug felt the consequences of his sin. In God's world, sin is always paid for. The good news for Christians is that we don't have to worry that God will make us pay eternally for our mistakes. Because Jesus "took away the sin of the world" (John 1:29).

Jesus, thank you for paying for my sins. Forgive me when I do wrong. Amen.

THEME: SIN

In Case of Sin, Remember This

My dear children, I'm writing this to you so that you will not sin. But suppose someone does sin. Then we have one who speaks to the Father for us. He stands up for us. He is Jesus Christ, the Blameless One.

1 JOHN 2:1

"I didn't mean it, Mom," Julie cried. "I forgot!"

"I understand that," Mom answered. "But you know the rules. You shouldn't have gone to Mary's without telling me. Now you're grounded for a week."

Some mistakes are deliberate, like Doug's in yesterday's story. Julie's mistake happened because she forgot. Or maybe she wanted to forget!

What happens when we make a mistake in God's eyes? John says in 1 John 2:1 that Jesus is like a defense attorney. But he is better than that. He's also got an in with the Judge because he paid for our sins. Thus, he can always work things out with the Father.

Every time we sin, Jesus steps up to talk to his Father. And he says, "I paid for that one on the cross!" We may have a small punishment in this world, but God says it's forgiven in his eyes.

Praise you, God, for your forgiveness. I feel new inside today because of your love. In Jesus, amen.

THEME: SIN

Restore the Sinner

Brothers and sisters, what if someone is caught in a sin? Then you who are guided by the Spirit should correct that person. Do it in a gentle way. But be careful. You could be tempted too.

GALATIANS 6:1

"She lies, all the time," Erin said. "I hate it."

"You know what to do in such a situation?" her teacher asked.

"I guess just not be friends anymore."

"No, that's exactly what you shouldn't do."

Her teacher showed Erin Galatians 6:1. There it tells us to correct the person who has sinned. How? In a gentle way. And remember that you might be tempted with the same sin!

See that word *correct*. It means "bring him back to spiritual condition." When we see someone make a mistake, or even commit a sin, we shouldn't ignore them, hate them, or reject them. We are commanded to go tell them what has happened, and *correct* them.

I have a friend who lies all the time, Lord. You know her, and you can help her. Use me to be a means of good in her life. Amen.

THEME: SIN

When a Leader Sins

Elders who sin should be corrected in front of the other believers. That will be a warning to the others.

1 TIMOTHY 5:20

Sometimes a mistake is so serious, severe actions must be taken. For instance, when a leader sins, we can't overlook it. Or pretend it didn't happen. Or even go along with it.

Paul said in 1 Timothy 5:20 that elders should be corrected in front of the whole church. Why? So that everyone will be warned.

We hope this never happens to you. But in some cases, a sin is so bad, the rest of the church must be warned. Everyone must become watchful. When someone is rebuked in public, he will never forget it.

Of course, you can never rebuke someone flippantly. The church must go through a proper process outlined in Matthew 18:15–17. But each of us must beware: sin is serious. And everyone should take it seriously.

Help me, Father, to treat sin as serious. I praise you that you are helping me through your Word to live right. Amen.

THEME: SIN

Paid For: Past, Present, and Future

He himself carried our sins in his body on the cross. He did it so that we would die as far as sins are concerned. Then we would lead godly lives. His wounds have made you whole.

1 PETER 2:24

Where do our sins go? Does God write them down in a book? Do angels keep track of everything we do?

The Bible reveals that God does keep books (Revelation 20:12). But it also reveals that when we become Christians, God "wipes out" or "erases" every sinful thing we've ever done (or will do) that is in the book. Why does he do this? Because Jesus "carried our sins in his body on the cross" (1 Peter 2:24).

Jesus paid for every one of our sins—past, present, and future—when he died on the cross. Jesus stepped up and said, "Punish me in . . . (your name) place." Then God punished him, and it was finished. Psalm 103:12 says that God has separated us from our sins as "far as the east is from the west."

Sometimes I think my sins are always before your eyes, God. But I know now how far away you've put them. Thanks. In Jesus' name, amen.

THEME: SIN

When Your Sins Are Forgiven

Blessed are those whose lawless acts are forgiven. Their sins have been taken away.

PSALM 32:1

Remember when your mom or dad or sister or brother forgave you for something you did wrong? How did you feel?

If you were genuinely forgiven, you probably felt good. Like the whole thing was over. You had nothing more to worry about. No fear of getting caught. No more guilt. It was done. Finished. Buried.

That's a good feeling, isn't it? And that's exactly how God wants us to feel about our sins before him. David wrote in Psalm 32:1, "Blessed are those whose lawless acts are forgiven. Their sins have been taken away."

Blessed means "happy" or "fortunate." Happy is the person who has been forgiven for a wrong. Do you want to be free from guilt? Then go make your sin right and seek forgiveness. You will feel much better having done so.

Lord, right now I confess that I did _____. Please forgive me and cleanse me and help me not to do it again. Amen.

THEME: SIN

What If You Sin the Same Sin Again and Again?

We know that those who are children of God do not keep on sinning. The Son of God keeps them safe. The evil one can't harm them.

1 JOHN 5:18

Can a true Christian keep on doing the same sin over and over?

First John 5:18 tells us, "We know that those who are children of God do not keep on sinning." A true Christian will not keep on sinning willfully. Sooner or later, he'll change his behavior.

I remember the day I stopped using foul language. My nickname in college was "Guttermouth" because I had such a foul mouth. I wanted to stop using bad words, but I couldn't. Then I became a Christian. And one day, God said, "Shouldn't you stop cursing?" I agreed. Since then I have rarely had a problem with it.

The Spirit will point out your sin if you're really a Christian. And when he does, you'll listen. Maybe not at first. But soon. It doesn't mean you'll be perfect. But gradually the problem will disappear from your life. That's how the Spirit works in us.

Work in me now, Jesus, to take away all the sinful things I do. Amen.

THEME: SIN

Conviction unto Confession

I know the lawless acts I've committed. I can't forget my sin.

PSALM 51:3

What happens to a Christian when he or she commits a sin?

The Spirit of God begins to convict him. The Spirit speaks in that person's heart. He talks to that person through his conscience. The Spirit tries to persuade the person to change his mind ("repent") and admit that he was wrong.

King David of Israel is a good example. Remember what he did? He took another man's wife and then he had that man killed. From that point on, David tried to conceal his sins. But God spoke to a prophet, and that prophet went to David to expose him. When the prophet spoke, David was convicted. This is what he said later, "I know the lawless acts I've committed. I can't forget my sin" (Psalm 51:3).

When we sin, God will not just let us go. He wants us to stop sinning and admit our wrong. Is the Spirit of God convicting you about anything right now?

I feel convicted about _____, Lord. Will you forgive me and change me so I don't do it anymore? Amen.

THEME: CONFESSION

Act Quickly

Then I admitted my sin to you. I didn't cover up the wrong I had done.

After King David realized he had sinned against God, he acted quickly. He says in Psalm 32:5, "Then I admitted my sin to you. I didn't cover up the wrong I had done."

When we admit our sin—confess to and agree with God about what we've done—we find true freedom. God forgives the guilt of our sin.

Have you ever been pained by guilt feelings about something? It's not pleasant. The only way to deal with guilt is to confess it and make it right. Otherwise, we'll either go around feeling very unhappy, or we'll "harden" our hearts. That is, we'll push God away, and our heart will feel dead and empty inside.

Do you have any sins you need to confess to God? Why not make them right, right now?

There's one sin I hide from you, Master. You know what it is. Forgive me for it and enable me to stop it in my life. In Jesus, amen.

THEME: CONFESSION

Complete Cleansing

If we admit that we have sinned, he will forgive us our sins. He will forgive every wrong thing we have done. He will make us pure.

1 JOHN 1:9

The miracle of confession of sin is that God doesn't just clean us up from that sin. No, he cleans us of everything wrong we've done. He makes us new and whole inside. We feel free and lifted up.

This is what John tells us in 1 John 1:9: "If we admit that we have sinned, he will forgive us our sins. He will forgive every wrong thing we have done. He will make us pure."

Do you see what God does when we confess sin?

1. God doesn't get angry and reject us.
2. He forgives us. He puts the sin out of his mind.
3. He cleans up anything else we may have forgotten or overlooked.

That's some forgiveness, don't you think?

It's so hard, Father, to tell my mom and dad about this sin. But help me to confess it to them so I'll feel free again. Amen.

THEME: CONFESSION

confess to others

So admit to one another that you have sinned. Pray for one another so that you might be healed. The prayer of a godly person is powerful. It makes things happen.

JAMES 5:16

Stephanie's face looked long and tired. "What's wrong?" asked Mom.

"I feel bad," Stephanie answered.

"Why?"

"I did something wrong."

"Did you confess it?" Mom asked.

"Yes, but I still feel bad."

When we sin, often we still feel bad even though we've confessed. What should we do then? One of the best things is found in James 5:16: "So admit to one another that you have sinned. Pray for one another so that you might be healed."

Sometimes we need to confess our sin to the person we sinned against. And sometimes, we just need to tell a friend or a parent. Often, when they pray for us, we'll feel better on the spot. Why? Because God works through that person to help us receive his forgiveness.

I know I should pay back _____ for what I took from him, Father. Help me to do what's right in this matter. Amen.

THEME: CONFESSION

How to Confess a Sin

I said, "I will admit my lawless acts to the LORD." And you forgave the guilt of my sin.

PSALM 32:5

How do you confess a sin? Here are several steps.

First, deal with a specific sin. Don't talk in generalities. "Oh, Lord, forgive me for everything." No, you should mention specifically what you did wrong.

Second, admit what you did wrong. You need to understand why this was a sin. Admitting what was wrong about it will help you see that truth.

Third, talk to God about it in prayer. Speak to him. Kneel down by your bed, or in an empty room, wherever you are. Tell him what you think you did wrong.

Fourth, ask for his forgiveness.

Fifth, if necessary, go to the person you sinned against and admit to him you're sorry, too.

Sixth, you may have to pay back something to make the error right.

Taking these steps will not only make you feel better, they will clear the air between you, God, and others. You will be free to live again.

Teach me to confess everything I do wrong, Lord, so I can please you in everything. Amen.

THEME: CONFESSION

Confess It in Public—Sometimes

They stood where they were. They listened while the Levites read parts of the Scroll of the Law of the LORD their God. They listened for a fourth of the day. They spent another fourth of the day admitting their sins. They also worshiped the LORD their God.

NEHEMIAH 9:3

Sometimes just telling God your sin isn't enough. Sometimes telling your mom or dad or a friend isn't enough. Sometimes, what you have to do is confess your sin in public.

In Nehemiah 9:3, the Jews were convicted of sin as the Levites read the Law. As a result, they confessed their sin. In public.

When should you confess a sin in public—before your class, to your family, in front of the church? When your sin was a public sin. When everyone knows about it. If you got in a fight at church in front of the class, you should admit your wrong to the whole class.

It's the only way to feel right and get right with God and his people.

I need to confess my sin to some people I've hurt, Lord. Please help me to say the right thing. Amen.

THEME: CONFESSION

God Confesses to Knowing us

Those who overcome will also be dressed in white. I will never erase their names from the Book of Life. I will speak of them by name to my Father and his angels.

REVELATION 3:5

Did you know that even God confesses things?

Not sin, but look at what Jesus told the church in Sardis in Revelation 3:5 above. He would dress the overcomers in white. He would not erase their names from the Book of Life. And he would speak (or "confess") our names to God. He will tell God we belong to him.

One day, Jesus will "admit"—confess—to being your friend, your Savior, your Lord, to all of creation. Everyone will know that you belong to him.

Can you imagine it? All the bullies, bad people, and those who hurt you are gathered. They think you're a nobody, that you never counted.

And then Jesus steps up and says, "He's my friend. We're going to be together forever."

I can't wait till that happens. Can you?

I'm so glad Jesus is my friend, Father, and that he's never ashamed of me. Help me never to be ashamed of him. In Jesus, amen.

THEME: CONFESSION

A Tough Commandment

Do not steal.

EXODUS 20:15

The eighth commandment warns us not to steal. That covers everything from stealing from Mom's pocketbook or Dad's wallet, to stealing from your sister's piggy bank or your friend's room. In the eyes of God, stealing is evil. Why? Because it shows you don't trust God.

What does God want us to do instead? Pray. Ask him to supply what you need. Go to him with your questions and needs. Expect him to answer.

Stealing means that we don't trust God to give us what we need and want. We take matters into our own hands.

Have you stolen anything from a family member, a friend, or a schoolmate? Then return it, apologize, and ask their forgiveness. That's the only way to deal with "sticky fingers."

I've had "sticky fingers," Lord, and I need to make right some wrongs. Help me to do this without making excuses. In Jesus' name, amen.

THEME: STEALING

The Worst Thief of All Time

He didn't say this because he cared about the poor. He said it because he was a thief. Judas was in charge of the money bag. He used to help himself to what was in it.

JOHN 12:6

Did you know that one of Jesus' own disciples was a thief? Yes, Judas Iscariot, the disciple who betrayed Jesus, started sinning long before his worst deed. He "pilfered" from the money bag. Do you know what that means? He took a little here and a little there. Just enough to satisfy. Not enough to be noticed. Then he went out and bought whatever he wanted at the moment.

Sure, Judas probably didn't take a lot. It was just nickels, dimes, and quarters. But in the eyes of God it's all the same. Whether you wrongly take a penny or a million dollars, it's all stealing. And one day it will catch up with us.

Some of my friends steal, Father, shoplifting and taking from their parents. Help me to speak the truth to them. Amen.

THEME: STEALING

How to Avoid Stealing

Those who have been stealing must never steal again. Instead, they must work. They must do something useful with their own hands. Then they will have something to give to people in need.

EPHESIANS 4:28

When you steal, you do more than sin against God. You sin against yourself and others.

But God had a remedy for stealing. How can we get what we want? By working for it. Even you as a young boy or girl can do that. Wash the dishes. Mow the lawn. Rake up leaves. Vacuum the living room. If you don't know anything to do to earn money, ask your mom or dad. They'll come up with something.

Then you'll not only have money for yourself. If you meet someone with a need, you can help them out, too.

Help me to earn the money I need, Jesus, so I'm not tempted to steal. Amen.

THEME: STEALING

How to Please God Every Day

Here are some commandments to think about. "Do not commit adultery." "Do not commit murder." "Do not steal." "Do not want what belongs to others." These and other commandments are all included in one rule. Here's what it is. "Love your neighbor as you love yourself."

ROMANS 13:9

There's a much larger commandment than stealing. It's in the above passage. Can you find what it is?

Yes, it's "Love your neighbor as you love yourself." Why is this greater? Stealing is negative. Don't do it. Loving is positive. Do it. When you love your neighbors, you will not steal from them. And you will also help them, pray for them, care about them.

God wants us to do more than just not steal. He wants us to go all the way into love. When we do that, we truly please him.

There are people I just don't love, God. Change my heart and help me to reach out to them with your love. Amen.

How to Treat Your Leaders

Teach slaves to obey their masters in everything they do. Tell them to try to please their masters. They must not talk back to them. They must not steal from them. Instead, they must show that they can be trusted completely.

TITUS 2:9–10

Slaves don't have much fun, do they? Fortunately, slavery has been outlawed throughout most of the world. But back in Jesus' times, slavery was common. In fact, in the Roman Empire there were more slaves than regular people.

Many slaves hated their masters. They would do anything to hurt them, like steal. But when they became Christians, Paul told them to love and respect and obey their masters. Was this hard? You bet.

You have masters too—teachers, parents, coaches. Do you hate them, or love them? Do you obey? Do you steal from them?

God wants us to honor those over us. When we honor them, we honor God, too. And God promises to reward us for that!

Our leaders are not always right, Father, but they deserve my respect. Help me to speak respectfully of our president and others. In Jesus, amen.

THEME: STEALING

Payback Time

Suppose you steal an ox or a sheep. And suppose you kill it or sell it. Then you must pay back five head of cattle for the ox. Or you must pay back four sheep or goats for the sheep.

EXODUS 22:1

"I have to pay back twice what I stole?" cried the criminal.

"Yes," said the judge. "Just be thankful I'm not using the Bible to make this sentence."

What if you had to pay back twice what you stole? Wouldn't that be awful? Then you would not only be poorer than you were before you stole, but you'd have to make the money to pay it back—by lawful means!

In the Old Testament, though, look at what you had to repay. For cattle, you paid back five times what you stole. For sheep, it was four times. Why did God do this? To keep people from stealing! They knew if they got caught, they were in big, BIG trouble.

God's laws are not to scare or hurt us. They're to keep us from harm. Obey God's laws and you will be blessed.

I know what your law says, Father. Now help me to live it out. Amen.

THEME: STEALING

Where to Store up Riches

Do not put away riches for yourselves on earth. Moths and rust can destroy them. Thieves can break in and steal them. Instead, put away riches for yourselves in heaven!
MATTHEW 6:19–20

When we steal, we want something. More money. A better toy. A Nintendo game. A football. A Barbie doll.

But Jesus warns us in the above passage that storing up things for ourselves is foolish. Why? Because it can easily be taken away. Moths eat clothing. Rust destroys metal. Thieves take money.

Instead of stealing, God advises us to put away treasure in heaven. What does that mean? Put your life into things that last. What is that? Friends. Family. Church. Love. Goodness. Kindness. Peace.

When you invest in the right things, you get to keep them forever.

Teach me to invest in the things that last, Lord, that I might always please you. Amen.

THEME: STEALING

The Hardest Commandment to Obey

Do not give false witness against your neighbor.

EXODUS 20:16

In a class of third, fourth, and fifth graders, the teacher asked what the hardest commandment was to obey. The class answered, "Do not lie."

"Why?" the teacher asked.

"Because it's so easy to do," one of the kids said.

Yes, it is easy. Lying sometimes just seems to "happen." You're asked if you finished your homework. You haven't. But you don't want to get into trouble. So you say, "Oh, hours ago!"

It can happen so many ways. We can lie about what we did or didn't do. About our friends. About our grades, our family, our use of time. It's so easy.

But it's wrong. God doesn't want us to lie. Why? Because it hurts him, it hurts others, and it hurts us.

Telling the truth takes effort. But it can be done. If you'll just try.

God who is true, teach me to speak truth always. In Jesus' name, amen.

THEME: LYING

Lying Affects Everyone

So each of you must get rid of your lying. Speak the truth to your neighbor. We are all parts of one body.

EPHESIANS 4:25

Imagine this situation. You smash your finger with a hammer. At first it hurts. But then your hand says, "Oh, it's not hurt. The hammer really missed." Your stomach says, "I'm okay. So don't worry about it." And your brain says, "I didn't see it happen, so it couldn't have happened."

Wouldn't that be crazy? But God says that's what it's like in the church when people lie. We're all part of Jesus' body. When we lie to one another, it's like a hand telling a hurt foot the hurt didn't happen. Or an eye telling an ear, "No one heard that!"

When we lie, we hurt the church. Its reputation with outsiders. Its friendship within itself. Its closeness. When we tell the truth, though, God blesses everyone in the church.

Bless our church, Father, and make us speakers of the truth. All the time. In every place. Amen.

THEME: LYING

How God Deals With Liars

You destroy those who tell lies. LORD, you hate murderers and those who cheat others.

PSALM 5:6

Jay was playing with matches. He got caught. When his dad asked him where he got the matches, Jay made up a story. "Tommy bought them for me," Jay said.

To his horror, Jay's dad said, "I guess I'll have to go talk to Tommy's dad."

That night Dad did. And he found out that his son had actually given the matches to Tommy! When he came home, he sat his son down and had a serious conversation with him. And then he grounded his son for a week.

When we tell lies, God has ways of letting the truth come out. When it does, we face the results. Sometimes those results are not pleasant. But discipline and being grounded are God's ways of stopping us from doing the same sin again.

The truth is: Tell the truth, and you won't have to worry about being caught!

Father, the other day I told a lie. It was a little one. But I shouldn't have done it. Forgive me and help me to tell the truth. In Jesus, amen.

THEME: LYING

How Would You Like to Be Homeless?

No one who lies and cheats will live in my house. No one who tells lies will serve me.

PSALM 101:7

When Cain killed his brother Abel, God asked him what had happened. He lied and said, "How should I know? Am I my brother's keeper?" God punished Cain for his murder and his lying with homelessness. He would never have a real home again. He would wander the earth without a place to rest his head.

One thing that happens when we lie is that we become like Cain. People avoid us. Friends stay away. Family tries to be supportive, but they don't trust you.

You become homeless. God also says that liars will not be allowed in his house.

Lying is such a dreadful thing. It hurts so many people. Ask yourself: Is there anything you've lied about? Can you make it right? Can you apologize?

If so, don't hesitate. Get it fixed now.

It's so hard to go and apologize for that lie, Lord. Help me, I pray, to make right what I did wrong. In Jesus' name, amen.

THEME: LYING

A Mouth Full of Sand

Food gained by cheating tastes sweet to you. But you will end up with a mouth full of sand.

PROVERBS 20:17

Have you ever been to the beach and gotten sand in your mouth? Yuck! Icky!

God says that's what happens when we cheat and lie.

A girl liked to shoplift. She snuck items into her purse. Then she walked out of stores without paying.

She didn't get caught for a long time. But one day, as she took a candy bar, she got caught. Store security nabbed her. They called home, and her parents had to come to the store to get her.

She said, "The moment I got caught, that candy looked awful!"

She got God's kind of sand in her mouth. In more ways than one.

Lord, I don't want to be a shoplifter. Help me to be honest in all my dealings with stores. In Jesus, amen.

THEME: LYING

Lying Friends

I don't spend time with people who tell lies. I don't keep company with pretenders.

PSALM 26:4

Alex stood out behind the church with his new friend, Mac. As they hid in a corner, Mac pulled out a cigarette. "Ever try one of these?" he said.

Alex shook his head, his eyes wide. Mac lit it and puffed. Then he handed it to Alex. "Take a drag," Mac said. "It's cool."

Just as Alex put the cigarette up to his lips, the church janitor came around the corner. "Hey, what's going on here?" the man said.

He took Alex and Mac into the church office. When Alex said Mac had brought the cigarettes, Mac denied it. Mac said, "He tried to get me to do it."

Alex was in bigger trouble than ever. But his biggest problem was Mac. Mac was the wrong kind of friend.

Watch out! Don't hang around with kids who lie. You'll only get into worse trouble than ever.

Lord, some of my friends tell lies all the time. Show me what to do and if I should continue to be friends with them. Amen.

THEME: LYING

The End of the Liar

Outside the city are the dogs and those who practice witchcraft. Outside are also those who commit sexual sins and murder. Those who worship statues of gods, and everyone who loves and does what is false, are outside too.

REVELATION 22:15

Some people get reputations as liars. Everyone knows they lie. Such a person was Tara. She lied about her family. She said, "My aunt is rich and promises to give me a million dollars when I grow up." She lied about where she got her clothes. "Oh, I wouldn't shop there. I get all my clothes at ..." She lied about what she did, who she knew, and everything else. Soon, everyone knew she was a liar.

It's sad. Sometimes people break the cycle. They become Christians. They start telling the truth. But some people never stop lying. God says their end is pitiful and horrible.

If you've been lying about things, stop. There's nothing that pleases God, parents, and people like someone who tells the truth.

At all costs, Father, make me a speaker of truth and not a liar. Because of who you are, I trust you to change me inside and outside. Amen.

THEME: LYING

Day-by-Day Honesty

An honest witness tells the truth. But a dishonest witness tells lies.

PROVERBS 12:17

Being honest is a day-by-day thing. You have to do it every day. It only takes a few dishonest moments to earn a bad reputation.

One of the first ways to be honest is simply telling the truth about what you've seen and known. For instance, Travis saw his friend Walt steal a CD from another friend, Bill. On the way home Travis said to Walt, "I saw what you did."

"What?"

"Took the CD."

"I did not!"

"I saw you, Walt," Travis said, looking him in the eye.

Walt looked away. "I guess I should take it back," he admitted.

All it takes sometimes is the right nudge.

Let me learn to speak the truth, Lord, with gentleness and love. In Jesus, amen.

THEME: HONESTY

When People Criticize

People who don't believe might say you are doing wrong. But lead good lives among them. Then they will see your good works. And they will give glory to God on the day he comes to judge.

1 PETER 2:12

"LeAnn is such a goody-goody," Carla said to Judy. "But I'll bet she does everything we do. She just does it when no one sees."

LeAnn overheard Carla, and she felt angry. She really didn't do the things they did, even when she knew she wouldn't be caught. But what could she do?

Some days later, LeAnn's friends came over to see her. Her mom let them in, and they went up to her bedroom. Just as they arrived, LeAnn dropped a lamp and broke it. "Oh . . . ," LeAnn started to say, then corrected herself. "Guess I'll just have to clean up."

Later Carla said to Judy, "Did you hear LeAnn? She didn't even swear!"

Judy laughed. "I know. I guess she really doesn't do the stuff we do."

You just never know who's watching!

Let me be found to be a person who does good, Jesus. Everywhere I go. Amen.

THEME: HONESTY

No Cheating Here!

Use honest scales and honest weights. Use honest dry measures. And use honest liquid measures. I am the LORD your God. I brought you out of Egypt.

LEVITICUS 19:36

A lady stood in the butcher shop and asked for a large chicken. The butcher put a chicken on the scales. It weighed three pounds. The lady said, "Do you have anything bigger?" He went back to the refrigerator and saw that was his last chicken. But he wanted to sell the lady what he had, so he took the same chicken, put a small weight in the neck opening, and weighed it. Four pounds.

"Oh, well," the lady said, "give me both of them!"

Caught! How embarrassing.

One of the easiest ways to be dishonest is to give someone less than they asked or paid for. Mowing the lawn, but leaving a dry patch uncut. Cleaning your room by shoving stuff under the bed.

An honest person does right. Every time.

Sometimes I'm sneaky, Lord, and I know that's wrong. Show me how to be straight and honest. In Jesus' name, amen.

THEME: HONESTY

What Would You Do?

Kings are pleased when what you say is honest. They value people who speak the truth.

PROVERBS 16:13

Barry saw the whole accident. His uncle was drunk again. He sideswiped a neighbor's car. When he saw Barry was the only witness, he stopped and said, "You tell anyone about this, boy, I'll beat you senseless."

The police came by for questioning. At first Barry was afraid to tell. He didn't want to get beat up. But finally he knew right was right. He told the officer, "My uncle did it. And he told me not to tell, or he'd beat me."

The policeman patted Barry on the back. "You did what was right, son. We'll make sure your uncle doesn't hurt you."

People in authority over us—teachers, policemen, firemen—all need to know the truth. When we speak the truth, we please them. And God, too.

My friend, _____, threatened me if I told the truth, Father. You know what will happen, so protect me, and help me do what's right. Amen.

THEME: HONESTY

Sent on a Mission

Moses, the servant of the LORD, sent me from Kadesh Barnea to check out the land. . . . I brought back an honest report to him. I told him exactly what I had seen.

JOSHUA 14:7

Remember how Joshua and the eleven other spies scoped out the land of Israel? And ten of the spies were afraid of what they saw? The people there were mighty and tough-looking. But Joshua and Caleb believed God would fight with them. Joshua gave his report, but the other ten prevailed. As a result, Israel wandered for the next forty years in the wilderness as a punishment for not trusting God.

Giving an honest report—whether it's in school, on a sports team, or just telling about a situation you witnessed—is important in God's eyes. Honest people don't say too little. They don't shut up when people are against them. No, they trust God.

And God gets them through. He'll get you through too.

I haven't always spoken up when kids talked about Jesus in school, Lord. I was afraid, but help me to be bold. Amen.

THEME: HONESTY

My Chance at Revenge

Don't pay back evil with evil. Be careful to do what everyone thinks is right.

ROMANS 12:17

Many movies and books are about revenge. We want to see the good guy get the bad guy back. For that reason, such stories are often thrilling and fun.

But what does God say about getting revenge? In the above passage, he wants us not to repay evil with evil. Instead, we should do right even if people think we're idiots.

Like Fran and Josie. Sisters. Josie had forgotten Fran's birthday in June. Now it was Josie's birthday in November. Would Fran get her sister back by not giving her a present?

No, instead, Fran gave Josie the best present she could find: a video game Josie had wanted for a year.

What do you think happened? Everyone not only praised Fran, but Josie herself decided never to forget her sister's birthday again.

Revenge is never the way to go. Do what's right, and you'll end up a winner.

I've been tempted to take revenge, Lord, but I know it's wrong. Help me instead to forgive. In Jesus, amen.

THEME: HONESTY

Do Right Every Chance You Get

We are trying hard to do what is right in the Lord's eyes and in the eyes of people.

2 CORINTHIANS 8:21

A preacher once told his children's class, "Do what's right every chance you get, and you will find that people do right to you, too."

A boy named Kit decided to see if it was true. He began in his fifth-grade class to do the right and good thing all the time. Kids began to know him as a guy who could be trusted. Over the years, they came to him with their problems. They asked for his advice. They went out of their way to make friends with him. He told them the same thing his preacher had told him: "Do what's right, and people will do right to you."

When it was time to graduate from high school, there were parties all over town. Kit was invited to ten of them! He had so many friends, he didn't know which parties to choose from. All through his life, he found people who liked and admired him. Why? Because of one thing: he did right. Even when it hurt.

Let everyone in our church do right this week, Lord, even when it hurts. I pray this in Jesus' name, amen.

THEME: HONESTY

How to Treat a Trial

You will face all kinds of trouble. When you do, think of it as pure joy. Your faith will be put to the test. You know that when that happens it will produce in you the strength to continue.

JAMES 1:2–3

Trials happen. Bad things come to everyone. Christians cannot avoid having troubles.

But how does a Christian respond to such trouble? With joy. Why? Because it's a chance to grow. It's an opportunity to become a little more like Jesus. It's a time to learn and develop as spiritual people.

When Ryan got sick from cancer, everyone thought he'd be angry and hard to get along with. But instead, he said he trusted God for whatever came and he even praised God. "Why?" his friends asked. Ryan answered, "It's not easy, but I really believe God is in charge, and I trust him to do what is right."

Trials are a chance to please the Lord with your faith. So how are you doing today?

Father, I don't always act joyful when bad times come. Help me to see your hand behind the trials. In Jesus, amen.

THEME: TRIALS

Jesus Knows What It's Like

God has made everything. He has acted in exactly the right way. He is bringing his many sons to share in his glory. To do so, he has made the One who saved them perfect because of his sufferings.

HEBREWS 2:10

How did God make Jesus perfect? By putting him through trials.

Did you realize that? One of the reasons Jesus went through so many hard times on earth was because his Father was making him perfect. God does the same thing for us. He develops us spiritually by putting us through tough circumstances. How does this perfect us? When we go through hard times, we learn patience, kindness, goodness, and loyalty.

Trials are a tool. God uses them to shape us into the image of Christ. Just as a sculptor cuts the marble with the chisel, so God chisels us with trials.

It's the only way we'll become what he wants to make of us.

You're making me like Jesus, Lord, and I appreciate that. Let me see trials and troubles as your tools to shape me. Amen.

THEME: TRIALS

Suffering for the Message of Jesus

So don't be ashamed to give witness about our Lord. And don't be ashamed of me, his prisoner. Instead, join with me as I suffer for the good news. God's power will help us do that.

2 TIMOTHY 1:8

It was reading time at school. Lydia pulled out her children's Bible and began to read. When she did, the girl next to her snickered. The teacher asked what was going on. When Lydia showed her the Bible, the teacher became angry.

"You know you're not supposed to bring that to school." She took the Bible away.

Over time, Lydia's parents took the issue to court. Lydia's face and name were on the front pages of the paper. One day, she said to her dad, "What good does all this do?"

He showed her the passage above. Sometimes people who want to live for Jesus will be persecuted and hated. But don't worry about it. God promises to reward those people beyond anything they can imagine.

I want to stand up for you, Jesus. In school. In church. On the playground. Help me to be strong. Amen.

THEME: TRIALS

Serving Even Though It Hurts

I served the Lord with tears. I served him even though I was greatly tested by the evil plans of the Jews.

ACTS 20:19

When the apostle Paul served God on his trips around the world, he was often hated and harmed. People whipped him. Several times he was stoned. He was shipwrecked. Beaten with rods. Rejected. Thrown out of cities.

It's amazing when you read it. Yet Paul never gave up. Why? Because he knew the power of Jesus and his message. He knew God would use it for good.

You may be persecuted if you stand up for Jesus, too. Kids might laugh at you. Or hit you. Or reject you.

But take heart. God will be with you in every trial along the way.

I've never been hated because of my love for Jesus, God. But I hope you'll help me to stay strong even if I am. In Jesus' name, amen.

THEME: TRIALS

All Part of a Plan

We sent our brother Timothy to give you strength and hope in your faith. He works together with God in spreading the good news about Christ. We sent him so that no one would be upset by times of testing. You know very well that we have to go through them.

1 THESSALONIANS 3:2–3

Did you know that God has planned that you go through trials? Yes, Paul tells us that he "had to go through" them. In other translations of the Bible it says he was "destined" for those trials.

Now why would God destine us to go through trials? Aren't they bad? Aren't they difficult? Don't they make life more painful?

In some ways. But remember what God is trying to do. He wants to make us like Jesus on the inside. That means attitudes and actions that are patient, kind, good, faithful, peaceful, and loving.

Next time you face a difficult trial, tell yourself this: God is making me a little more like Jesus.

I pray for all those Christians facing trials today, Father. Strengthen them and let them know you're with them in a special way. In Jesus, amen.

THEME: TRIALS

God to the Rescue

The Lord knows how to keep godly people safe in times of testing.

2 Peter 2:9

Have you ever watched a Superman movie? What happens? A disaster strikes. Clark Kent, mild-mannered reporter, hears about it. He steps into an empty room. He rips off his suit. Then he blasts out of a window and flies to the rescue.

Did you know God is sort of like that? No, not that he wears a blue and red suit with a big G on the chest. Nor does he fly around. But he's with us at all times and he's prepared to help us. In fact, he has planned exactly how he will rescue us out of the trial and get us past it. He knows just what to do.

That's comforting, isn't it? It means no matter where you are, no matter what the situation, God is planning to help you through it. He'll give you strength to face the trial, wisdom to solve the problem, and determination to see it through.

That's tremendous help, the kind we all need, the kind God gives us every day.

Keep me safe during this time of testing, Lord. Thank you that you are with me. Amen.

THEME: TRIALS

Not Even Worth Comparing

What we are suffering now is nothing compared with the glory that will be shown in us.

ROMANS 8:18

Whenever you face difficult times, there's something God always wants us to do. Compare it with what he tells us will happen in heaven.

What's going to happen in heaven? We'll reign with Jesus. Everyone will be perfect. No more sin. No more wars. No more suffering. God will wipe every tear from our eyes. We'll see him face-to-face. We'll reign forever.

Scripture hasn't revealed much more about heaven. Why? Perhaps because it's so incredible, it's literally indescribable. We'll just have to wait to get there to see for ourselves. Whatever it's like, though, Paul says that no matter how bad it gets down here, we shouldn't worry about it. The glory ahead will make it all worthwhile.

Keep my eyes on heaven, Lord, and get them off the things down here. Let me not be bothered by troubles, but let me be built up by them. Amen.

THEME: TRIALS

Don't Complain About It, Expect It!

In fact, everyone who wants to live a godly life in Christ Jesus will be treated badly.

2 TIMOTHY 3:12

Sandy looked like she was about to cry.

"What's the matter, honey?" her mother asked.

"Kids are saying nasty things about me," Sandy answered. Her lip trembled. "They're saying I think I'm too good for everyone."

"Because you're a Christian?"

"Yes. And they say a lot of other bad things, too."

Sandy's mother sat down next to her. "You know what the Bible says about it, honey?"

"No."

"Let me show you." Her mom showed her 2 Timothy 3:12. "It happens to all of us. It's part of belonging to Jesus. The world hates him, so it hates us."

"So then it's kind of a good thing," Sandy said brightly.

"Exactly!"

I pray for people who hate Christians, Jesus. Soften their hearts and help them come to you in faith. Amen.

THEME: PERSECUTION

A Badge of Honor

The apostles were full of joy as they left the Sanhedrin. They considered it an honor to suffer shame for the name of Jesus.

ACTS 5:41

Do you know what happened to Peter and John before this verse? They were whipped with a cat-o'-nine-tails. This was a whip with three to nine leather strands. Imbedded in the strands were bits of metal, bone, and stone. When you were whipped with one, your back and legs were ripped to shreds.

But Peter and John didn't weep or complain. They rejoiced that they had "suffered shame for the name of Jesus." They saw it as a badge of honor.

When people put you down or hate you, especially because you're a Christian, don't fret. Don't cry. Don't complain and be angry at God. Rejoice. Because it's Jesus they really hate. And to identify you as one of his is a great honor.

Sometimes the other kids hate me because I am a Christian, Lord. Fill me with faith and help me to be strong no matter what. Amen.

THEME: PERSECUTION

Jesus Won the Battle

I have told you these things, so that you can have peace because of me. In this world you will have trouble. But cheer up! I have won the battle over the world.

JOHN 16:33

Living in this world is tough. People sometimes hate us. For reasons like the color of our skin, the family we're from, our country, our accent, or our religion. It's not right. It's not fair. But that's the way it often is.

What should you do at such times? Cheer up, Jesus says. Why? Because he has gained a great victory over the world. In other words, he has already dealt with the world. One day, when we're with him in his home, the world will seem a distant, foolish place.

Yes, in this world we have a lot of trouble. But stop worrying. Jesus is preparing for us a new place where no one will ever mistreat another again!

I've seen people be mistreated because of their religion, Father. Work in our world to help us love and care for those who are different. Amen.

THEME: PERSECUTION

Put Them to Shame with Your Good Deeds

Live so that you don't have to feel you've done anything wrong. Some people may say evil things about your good conduct as believers in Christ. If they do, they will be put to shame for speaking like that about you.

1 PETER 3:16

How do you put people to shame by doing good?

The girls at school often teased Nicole because she didn't swear, lie, or cheat. Barbara was particularly mean to her. But Nicole had a good attitude. She knew Jesus would give her a chance to do good sometime.

One day Barbara came into class looking unhappy. No one paid much attention. But Nicole sat down next to her at lunch. She offered Barbara a cupcake and asked her what was wrong. Barbara said her parents were getting a divorce. Nicole listened and offered some advice. Afterwards, Barbara and Nicole became good friends.

That's a simple story, but true. It happens many times to Christians. When you do good to the people who are mean to you, they often stop being mean.

Help me to treat _____ with respect, even though they don't like me, Jesus. Maybe you'll even help me win them to faith in you. In Jesus' name, amen.

THEME: PERSECUTION

The Message Gives us Joy

We and the Lord were your examples. You followed us. You suffered terribly. Even so, you welcomed our message with the joy the Holy Spirit gives.

1 THESSALONIANS 1:6

Sometimes the gospel of Jesus is called the "good news." That's what it means in the original language. But why is it good news?

Because it tells us we can get rid of our guilt forever.

Because it assures us we have a home in heaven.

Because it says we'll live forever.

Because it offers us God's friendship.

Because it gives us hope that Jesus will go with us through everything.

Those are just a few of the things God does when we believe the gospel. That's why we don't worry when others hurt us. The message assures us this will all be over one day and we'll be free and happy forever.

Father, I look forward to the day when we walk with you perfectly. Come quickly, Lord Jesus. Amen.

THEME: PERSECUTION

Lead Good Lives

People who don't believe might say you are doing wrong. But lead good lives among them. Then they will see your good works. And they will give glory to God on the day he comes to judge.

1 PETER 2:12

The best way to stop nasty people is to do good to them. They may say bad things about us. But when we do good all the time, people know better.

"Oh, that's not true," Calvin said to Jerry. "Todd never lies. I know."

Jerry said, "I bet he steals stuff then."

"No," Calvin said. "In fact, he even stopped me once when I wanted to punch someone. And I would have been caught."

"I hate him!" Jerry said.

"Then you hate him for the wrong reasons," Calvin said.

It's true. Sometimes people hate for all the wrong reasons. It's the way this world is. But others will defend us. If we live good lives.

Make me a truly good person, Lord. Let me praise you by my thoughts, words, and deeds. Amen.

THEME: PERSECUTION

Nothing Can Take Him Away from Us

Who can separate us from Christ's love? Can trouble or hard times or harm or hunger? . . . No! In all these things we will do even more than win! We owe it all to Christ, who has loved us.

ROMANS 8:35, 37

Can anything take Christ's love away from you?

No! Nothing! Christ's love is so strong, so big, so everlasting, that it can never leave us.

Isn't that wonderful? It means no matter where you are, Jesus' love is there. It means no matter what you've done wrong, Jesus still loves you infinitely. It means no matter how far you've gone astray, Jesus is still there.

His love is high. We cannot reach over it.

His love is low. We cannot dig under it.

His love is wide. We cannot go around it.

His love is right here. We cannot escape it.

That's amazing love!

Thanks for loving me, Jesus. I only hope I can love you the same way in return. In you, amen.

THEME: PERSECUTION

Lots of Trouble

There are more troubles all around me than I can count. My sins have caught up with me, and I can't see any longer. My sins are more than the hairs of my head. I have lost all hope.

PSALM 40:12

This world is full of trouble. Job once said, "Man is born for trouble!" Being a Christian doesn't mean you have no problems. It might even mean that you have more. Why? Because you have all the normal troubles people get. Plus, you have some troubles simply because you're a Christian.

The person talking in the verse above had many problems. But throughout the psalm he reminds himself that God answered every time he called on him.

No matter how great your problems, remember: God is there. He's ready to help. Turn to him. Expect him to help. Look to him for answers and hope.

He promises you will never be disappointed.

No matter what troubles I have, Father, I trust you. Thank you for being with me in everything. In Jesus' name, amen.

THEME: TROUBLE

Save Me, Lord!

But when Peter saw the wind, he was afraid. He began to sink. He cried out, "Lord! Save me!"

MATTHEW 14:30

Peter was in the boat with the other disciples. A storm blew up. Their boat was pounded by waves. And then they all saw something: Jesus, walking on the water!

At first, they thought he was a ghost. But when they saw it was Jesus, Peter said, "If it's really you, Lord, let me come to you on the water."

Jesus told Peter to come. As Peter got out there, he looked around. The waves lashed at him. The wind raked at his face. Spray peppered his face. And he forgot Jesus was there. He began to sink. That's when he cried out, "Save me, Lord."

Problems are like that. Sometimes you do something for the Lord, and suddenly everything seems to go wrong. But God's promise is Jesus is there. And he will save you.

Do you believe that?

It must have been cool to walk on water with you, Jesus. But I know a greater miracle: walking with you every day. Thank you. Amen.

THEME: TROUBLE

Comfort for Those With Problems

He comforts us in all our troubles. Now we can comfort others when they are in trouble.

2 CORINTHIANS 1:4

Have you ever had someone say to you, "Yeah, I had that problem once. And this is what I did."

Or, "You know, I have a friend who had that happen to him. Would you like to talk to him and see how he got out of it?"

Do you know one reason you have problems? It's so that you can help others when they have similar problems!

Yes, one reason God gives you problems is so you can help others. What you learn while you have the problem is helpful. Your advice can guide someone else through his difficulty.

Nothing that happens to us is lost. God uses everything. And if we're smart, we'll learn to use everything, too.

Dear Lord, help me learn to comfort others. In Jesus, amen.

THEME: TROUBLE

uSe Your Head

There's a proper time and way for people to do everything. That's true even though they might be suffering greatly.

ECCLESIASTES 8:6

"Hey," Scott's dad yelled. "That's not the way to do it."

Scott kicked his bike chain again. "I can't fix it!"

His dad walked over. "There's a proper way to fix this, Scott," he said. "And if you don't do it the right way, it won't work."

"I know, but I don't know how to do it."

"Well, let me show you."

There's a proper time and way for people to do things, as the above Scripture says. When you have problems, the way to deal with them is not to jump in and start swinging. It's to . . .

> think it through
> make a plan
> do it.

Isn't that the smart way?

Lord, let me think through what I'm doing. Fill me with your wisdom. In Jesus' name, amen.

THEME: TROUBLE

God Delivers

Those who do what is right may have many troubles. But the LORD saves them from all of them.

PSALM 34:19

When you have problems, you may be tempted to solve them the wrong way. How?

> If you're caught doing something wrong, you may lie to get out of it.
> If you're hungry, you might steal.
> If you're angry, you might swear.

All those are the wrong ways of dealing with problems. When we do right, though, God supports us. He saves us out of our troubles. He delivers us.

Which would you rather do? Have a problem, lie, or steal to get out of it, and lose God's blessing? Or, have a problem, do what is right, and get God's blessing, too?

The answer should be fairly simple.

I want your blessing, Father. Show me your way to solve problems. Amen.

THEME: TROUBLE

Watch What You Say

Those who are careful about what they say keep themselves out of trouble.

PROVERBS 21:23

What is probably the biggest way most of us get into trouble? When we let our big mouths do the talking!

Isn't that true? When we mouth off, or get nasty, or say the wrong things, we get into worse trouble. The mouth can be very bad that way.

What's the solution? Be careful what you say. Think before you speak. Take some time and wait before answering a taunt or an insult. Be slow to speak, slow to anger, and quick to hear, James said.

It's really not hard. It's just a matter of controlling your tongue. And after all, who is in control of your tongue? You!

Help me, Lord, to control my tongue and think before I speak. Amen.

THEME: TROUBLE

Great Glory Ahead

Our troubles are small. They last only for a short time. But they are earning for us a glory that will last forever. It is greater than all our troubles.

2 Corinthians 4:17

Monday: Tess lost her Giga Pet.

Tuesday: She looked all day but couldn't find it.

Wednesday: In school, she cried twice when she saw other kids with Giga Pets.

Thursday: She found her pet in the wood bin. Her brother had dropped it there and forgotten about it.

Isn't that how a lot of problems in life go? One day it starts. Two days later, it's over. Or even less.

Certainly there are many longer-lasting problems. But the fact is that every problem is storing up glory for us. What's that? Praise and compliments from God in heaven about how we handled our problems. So let's all hope you get much glory when you get there!

I don't know what you'll say about me when I get to heaven, Lord, but help me now to do the things that will win your praise. In Jesus, amen.

THEME: TROUBLE

Becoming Like a Tree

I will bless those who trust in me.... They will be like a tree that is planted near water. It sends out its roots beside a stream.... It does not worry when there is no rain. It always bears fruit.

JEREMIAH 17:7–8

Worry is a bad thing. It ruins our waking hours. It sends acid through our guts. It causes good people to fear and fall.

But people who trust in the Lord don't need to worry about anything. He blesses them. He plants their roots deep, like a tree by a stream. Even when it doesn't rain, when the droughts come, it doesn't worry. God fills its boughs with fruit.

Worry is distrusting God about the future. For the Christian, the future is already secure. We know God will

> be there with us.
> go ahead of us and prepare the way.
> clean up behind us.

So what's to worry about?

Sometimes I worry, Jesus. Help me to learn to trust you for and in everything. In your name, amen.

THEME: WORRY

Jesus on Worry

I tell you, do not worry. Don't worry about your life and what you will eat or drink. And don't worry about your body and what you will wear. Isn't there more to life than eating? Aren't there more important things for the body than clothes?

MATTHEW 6:25

Jesus didn't want his listeners to worry. He assured them in the Sermon on the Mount that there really was nothing to worry about. Why? Because God would provide for them. God would meet their needs. All they had to do was ask.

Such truth still holds today. Mark Twain once said that he worried about a great many things that never happened. Rarely do our worries come true. And yet they take our time and our lives away.

The answer to worry is trust. Trust in the Lord. When we do that, we find he opens the doors we need for whatever problem we have.

I trust you, Father, because I know you love me and you're wise. You can do everything needed to bless my life. Thank you, in Jesus' name, amen.

THEME: WORRY

What Could Happen Tomorrow?

So don't worry about tomorrow. Tomorrow will worry about itself. Each day has enough trouble of its own.

MATTHEW 6:34

What's the biggest thing most of us worry about? Tomorrow. What might happen. Where we'll go. What could go wrong.

Do you worry about tomorrow? Jesus says, "Stop. Put God's kingdom first and everything will be given to you that you need."

God blesses those who serve him. Can you imagine a loving parent who would let his child go hungry? Or without clothes?

God is like a loving parent. But even more. He's all-powerful. He's wise. He's perfect. And he cares for us more than even a parent can. He knows what our needs are before we even ask him.

When you worry, stop and ask yourself: Does God care about me? Does he know about my situation? Can he help? Yes, yes, and yes. So what's to worry about?

You have the future laid out, Lord. You have my past forgiven. You are with me in the present. I don't need to worry about anything. Amen.

THEME: WORRY

Anxiety in the Heart

Worry makes your heart heavy. But a kind word cheers you up.

PROVERBS 12:25

Fred sat at his desk looking scared. His friend Katy asked what was wrong. "I'm worried I flunked the test," he said.

"Did you study?" she asked.

"Yes."

"Did you do your best?"

"Yes."

"Then you have nothing to worry about."

Fred looked at her angrily. "I still might have flunked."

"The test is over," Katy said. "If you studied and did your best, that's all that's expected of you. That's what my dad says."

Fred thought about it. Katy had a "kind word" and it cheered him up. Sometimes all you need when you're worried is for someone to say, "Hey, it'll be all right. Come on, I'll buy you an ice-cream cone." And all that worry goes away!

Work in _____, Jesus. She's worried about so many things. Help her to trust you. Amen.

THEME: WORRY

The Remedy for Worry

Don't worry about anything. Instead, tell God about everything. Ask and pray. Give thanks to him. Then God's peace will watch over your hearts and your minds because you belong to Christ Jesus.

PHILIPPIANS 4:6–7

This is a great verse for helping us with our worries. What does it teach us?

1. Stop worrying. Just tell yourself, "Enough. I won't think about this anymore." But that's not enough.
2. Tell God what's on your mind. Spill it out. Tell him what you're feeling, then ask, pray, and thank him for listening. Expect him to answer in a powerful way.
3. God will send you his peace. When we make our hearts talk to God, worry is forced out. God puts his peace in its place.

Are you worried? Follow these three steps. God has promised he'll answer quickly.

Lead me, Lord, to learn to see you working in everything. Work in my parents and help them to lead me. In Jesus' name, amen.

THEME: WORRY

What If ...?

But when they arrest you, don't worry about what you will say or how you will say it. At that time you will be given the right words to say.

MATTHEW 10:19

Have you ever played the "What if ..." game?

What if I lose the game?

What if I flunk fifth grade?

What if I don't get elected?

What if the police come and take my family away?

What if the world goes crazy and all the Christians are thrown into prison?

The "What ifs?" can get bigger and bigger and bigger. And the worry goes higher. But Jesus told his disciples they weren't to think about such things. In fact, what they were to think was that it could be a good thing. Why? Because it would be a chance for God to speak through you to unbelievers!

Now that's a switch, isn't it? Don't worry about problems because God will help you solve them. Wow!

I know you're helping me solve problems, Father. Every day I will listen for your voice. In Jesus, amen.

THEME: WORRY

A Prayer for Bedtime

God, see what is in my heart. Know what is there. Put me to the test. Know what I'm thinking. See if there's anything in my life you don't like. Help me live in the way that is always right.

PSALM 139:23–24

Sometimes this is called the worrier's prayer. A good time to leave your worries behind is at bedtime. Tomorrow is a new day. New things will happen. New solutions will appear for old problems.

When you've had a tough day, stop before bed and pray. "God, search my heart. Take a good look at it. Show me right now what's in it that's bad. Or worrisome. Or wrong. Then help me remove it."

It's a good way to end the day.

It's also a good way to begin one.

Jesus, let me begin the day with you. And let me end it with you too. Then you'll be part of everything. In you, amen.

Resist the Devil

So obey God. Stand up to the devil. He will run away from you.

JAMES 4:7

Ever hear quiet little voices in your mind urging you to do wrong things?

"Go ahead. Sock him in the face. He deserves it."

"Take the money. No one will know."

"It was okay to lie. Nobody got hurt."

"You need a good grade. So take a look at her paper. The teacher is looking the other way."

Our minds are amazing things. In them we can hear our conscience, our own thoughts, and also the still small voices of God and even the devil. Every one of those voices is trying to get our attention.

But God gave us a safeguard. Our conscience. It always tells us to do what's right. When you hear a thought that says to do wrong, resist it. Stand up to it. The devil will run when he sees you doing right.

I'd like to see the devil run, Lord. Help me to do right always. In Jesus, amen.

THEME: THE TEMPTER

The Roaring Lion

Control yourselves. Be on your guard. Your enemy the devil is like a roaring lion. He prowls around looking for someone to chew up and swallow.

1 PETER 5:8

Why does a lion roar when it's close to its prey? Because it wants to freeze its victim with fright. It doesn't want to work too hard to catch them. So it roars, thinking this will scare the prey into falling over.

Satan is like that, too. He prowls around looking for victims. He's especially hungry for Christians. Nothing pleases him more than a Christian who sins, knowing it's sin. He taunts. He caresses. He purrs. He roars. Anything to get us to do his will.

How do you deal with him? Be on guard. Watch. Be ready. When he comes, pray, quote Scripture, and even run. The devil wants you to sin. Any way you can avoid it will help you win.

Teach me your Word, Father, so I can use it to defeat the devil. In Jesus' name, amen.

THEME: THE TEMPTER

The Bread Caper

The tempter came to him. He said, "If you are the Son of God, tell these stones to become bread." Jesus answered, "It is written, 'People don't live only on bread. They also live on every word that comes from the mouth of God.'"

MATTHEW 4:3–4

When Jesus first started his ministry, he was tested by the devil. It happened in the wilderness. The first thing the devil did was taunt Jesus to make stones out of bread. Of course, Jesus as God could do this. But his Father wanted something else: that he *not* eat. So it would have been wrong to make bread out of stones at that time.

How did Jesus stop Satan in his tracks? He quoted Scripture. He used a verse that applied to the situation. And Satan gave up on that strategy.

There are two things necessary for us to defeat Satan: (1) know the Scriptures; (2) obey them.

If you do that, you will defeat Satan every time.

Help me to be on guard and watch for the tricks of the devil, Lord. Let me defeat him with your Word. Amen.

THEME: THE TEMPTER

Another Trick of the Devil

The devil took Jesus to the holy city. He had him stand on the highest point of the temple. "If you are the Son of God," he said, "throw yourself down. It is written, 'The Lord will command his angels to take good care of you. They will lift you up in their hands.'"

MATTHEW 4:5–6

When Satan first tempted Jesus, he just made a suggestion. But the second time, he actually quoted Scripture himself. But not all of it. Just the part that fit his plans.

How did Jesus reply? He said, "It is also written, 'Do not put the Lord your God to the test'" (Matthew 4:7).

Sometimes Satan will use Scripture against us. He tells us to "speak the truth," so we let it out with both barrels. He tells us to lie. Then when we lie, he comes and says, "Oooh, you sinned. Now God is against you."

Satan will do anything to stop us. But knowing the Bible well and obeying it, as Jesus did, stops him.

Father, let me know your Word and then obey it. Help me listen in church and to my parents. Amen.

THEME: THE TEMPTER

Everything You've Ever Dreamed Of

Finally, the devil took Jesus to a very high mountain. He showed him all the kingdoms of the world and their glory. "If you bow down and worship me," he said, "I will give you all of this."

MATTHEW 4:8–9

What if someone to said to you, "Ask for anything. I'll give you anything you want. All you have to do is this little thing in return ..."

Satan does that to us all the time.

"Just tell this little lie, and everything will be fine."

"All you have to do is cry, and your mom won't make you clean your room."

"Just listen to what Samantha says about Vern. He's your friend, sure, but it'll be interesting."

Oh, the devil has a million of them. How did Jesus handle this temptation? He said, "Get away from me, Satan! It is written, 'Worship the Lord your God. He is the only one you should serve'" (Matthew 4:10).

Jesus quoted Scripture and obeyed. Looks like knowing Scripture and obeying it is pretty important. Don't you think?

Make my eyes and my heart wise, Jesus, so I can beat the devil at his games. Amen.

THEME: THE TEMPTER

Putting the Devil on the Run

Put on all of God's armor. Then you can stand firm against the devil's evil plans.

EPHESIANS 6:11

In Ephesians 6:11–18, Paul talks about one of the more important things in Christian living: the armor of God. When a soldier goes into battle, he needs protection. He needs weapons. He needs a leader.

It's all there in Ephesians 6. Paul warns us to put on the armor so we can stand against the devil's plans. What does the devil want to do?

Make you sin.

Make you turn from God.

Make you give up the faith.

He starts with sin. If he gets you sinning enough, he figures he can then get you to turn from God. And his ultimate plan is to make you give up your faith. It all starts with little sins that get bigger and bigger.

What sins are you letting creep into your life? Confess them and stop them today. Or the devil will have you for lunch tomorrow.

Teach me to watch for the little sins, Lord. Teach me to do the things that please you. In Jesus' name, amen.

THEME: THE TEMPTER

God Will Deal with the Bad Guys

He grabbed the dragon, that old serpent. The serpent is also called the devil, or Satan. The angel put him in chains for 1,000 years.

REVELATION 20:2

Tough as the devil is, he's not so tough that God won't beat him. In the end, Satan will be grabbed by an angel and thrown into the pit. He'll stay there for a thousand years. At the end of that time, Revelation says he'll be let loose for a short time. And then he'll be confined in hell forever.

No matter how bad it gets, remember the devil has an end. God isn't going to let him roam around forever. All you have to do is wear the armor and fight him on a daily basis. God has the end well in hand.

Do you ever feel like it's a losing battle? Don't. The battle is already won and Satan knows his time is short. In fact, next time he comes around to tempt you, tell him exactly that. "Jesus is gonna deal with you, bud!"

That will make him very unhappy indeed.

Thank you, Jesus, for dealing with the devil once and for all. I trust you to lead me in the battle. Amen.

THEME: THE TEMPTER

First: Look to God!

I looked to the LORD, and he answered me. He saved me from everything I was afraid of.

PSALM 34:4

Fears can be terrible, mind-breaking realities. They cripple us. They stop us from taking the risks in faith so necessary for Christian living.

If you are afraid, the first thing you should do is look to the Lord. Yes, look. Put your eyes on him. Peer into his Word. Find truths that comfort you. Then latch onto them. God is faithful, and he will not allow us to be shamed.

What are you afraid of? Death? School? Failing? Sin? A bad mistake? A bully down the street? A sports situation? Your coach? Your mom? Your dad?

God says, "Look to me. I'll help. I'll save you from everything you're afraid of." It's a promise.

Try it.

Sometimes I'm afraid, Lord. I know I should trust you, but it's hard. Teach me to trust you in everything. Amen.

THEME: FEAR

No One Can Touch Me!

The Lord helps me. I will not be afraid. What can people do to me?

HEBREWS 13:6

"What's the matter, Nathan?" Dad asked.

"I'm afraid."

"Of what?"

"A kid."

"A bully?"

"Yeah."

Dad knelt down by his son. "Do you know what? That bully is in God's hands. And you're also in God's hands. So you don't have to be afraid. Do you think God is going to let you down?"

He won't! Every person in the universe is in God's hands. No one can do anything to another without God letting them. So trust in God, and he'll help you.

You are good, Father, and I trust you about _____, who's making trouble in my life. Work in him and change him. In Jesus' name, amen.

THEME: FEAR

The Spirit of Power and Love

God didn't give us a spirit that makes us weak and fearful. He gave us a spirit that gives us power and love. It helps us control ourselves.

2 TIMOTHY 1:7

When God made you a Christian, he didn't give you a "spirit"—your internal person—who is afraid and weak. No, that person is strong, loving, and self-controlled. Did you realize that?

God has given us all the equipment we need inside to overcome our fears. Our spirit is like a baseball bat. It's strong. It's hard. It won't break or bend. Swing that bat! Smack that ball! And run for first base!

God has given us a bat that we can trust. Our internal self, united with him, is powerful, loving, and in control. Let him take charge, and you can't help but beat any fears that strike.

I know I'm in your hands, Lord. They're good hands, and I look forward to whatever you're going to bring into my life today. In Jesus, amen.

No Fear in Love

There is no fear in love. Instead, perfect love drives fear away. Fear has to do with being punished. The one who fears does not have perfect love.

1 JOHN 4:18

Do you ever become afraid of facing God? Of judgment? Of going to hell, or anything like that?

If you're a Christian, this is the right approach to such questions: Does God love you? Yes! What kind of love does God love you with? Good love? Wise love? Kind love? Perfect love?

All of the above. But most of all, perfect love. God loves each one of us perfectly. That means if we believe in him he will never punish us. We never need fear that we'll pay eternally for our sins. Jesus paid for them all. We never need to fear he will let us go. Or give up on us. Or get mad and throw us out!

No, God loves us perfectly. And his love is forever!

Thank you for your assurance that you'll never desert me, Father. That gives me great hope for the future and today. Amen.

Sharing Your Faith

When I came to you, I was weak and afraid and trembling all over.

1 CORINTHIANS 2:3

One of the things that scares Christians the most is sharing their faith. We don't know whether the person we want to talk to will become angry, or hostile, or just indifferent. Since we never know what the response will be, we often fear the worst.

And then we don't share our faith.

Do you know where that fear is from? The devil. He cranks up our fear because he doesn't want us telling anyone about Jesus. Even Paul in the passage above was afraid of witnessing to the Corinthians. But he decided to "stuff" his fear and do it anyway.

Sometimes that's the only way to deal with fear. Stuff it: tell yourself to forget about it, and go on. Don't worry about the response. Worry about your responsibility before God!

I'm trying to deal with my fears, Jesus. But I need your help. Show me today how to work with one: _____. That's a biggie. In your name, amen.

THEME: FEAR

Fear of Getting Caught

If you do what is right, you won't need to be afraid of your rulers. But watch out if you do what is wrong!

ROMANS 13:3

One of life's biggest fears is of getting caught when you do wrong. You steal some money, tell a lie, or cheat on an exam. What happens? You're afraid. Maybe someone saw you. Maybe the teacher knows. Maybe your dad or mom will find out tonight!

If you're afraid of getting caught for doing wrong, God won't take away that fear. In fact, he has sent you that fear. It's called guilt. You have guilt because God wants you to stop and think about what you've done. He wants you to repent, to confess your sin, to make it right.

Have you done something wrong? Are you afraid of getting caught? Then go, confess what you did. Make it right. Then your fear will be gone forever.

Sometimes I'm afraid of getting caught when I've done something wrong, Lord. I know now that fear is from you. Forgive me and make me whole. Amen.

THEME: FEAR

Fear of Death

Jesus became a human like them in order to die for them. By doing that, he could destroy the one who rules over the kingdom of death. . . . Jesus could set people free who were afraid of death. All their lives they were held as slaves by that fear.

HEBREWS 2:14–15

The fear of death is strong. We don't want to die. We fight it, to our last breath.

The fear of death happens in two ways. People fear how they will die—will it be painful? And they wonder what will happen after death—will they go to heaven or hell?

For Christians, God gives two promises. First, he will be with us always. He will go with us through death. Second, he will welcome us to his kingdom. He assures us if we believe we're bound for heaven.

Does that help you in your fear of death?

Father, I don't think about death much. But sometimes it scares me. Thank you for your assurance you'll be there for me. In Jesus, amen.

THEME: FEAR

Are You True to the Lord?

When he arrived and saw what the grace of God had done, he was glad. He told them all to remain true to the Lord with all their hearts.

ACTS 11:23

Nothing pleases a spiritual leader more than to find his people true to the Lord. Are you true to the Lord? How do you know if you are?

A person who is true to the Lord . . .

obeys God's commands.
attempts great things for God in faith.
prays regularly.
reads and studies Scripture daily.
helps others as much as he can.
serves and gives the best he has.

Being true to the Lord is not hard. And it's the most rewarding thing we can do in life. Where are you in your relationship with God? Are you being true? What ways can you improve?

Let me be true to you, Jesus. Every day and every step of the way. In your name, amen.

THEME: COMMITMENT

A Man Who Was True

> "LORD, *please remember how faithful I've been to you. I've lived the way you wanted me to. I've served you with all my heart. I've done what is good in your sight." And Hezekiah cried bitterly.*

This is an interesting verse. In it, a faithful king of Israel, Hezekiah, has just been told he will die. Hezekiah is astounded and hurt. After all the good things he did for God, this is how he gets repaid?

But Hezekiah wasn't just an ordinary faithful king. Look at what he says of himself:

I've been faithful.
I've lived the way you wanted me to.
I've served you with all my heart.
I've done what is good in your sight.

That's a pretty impressive list. Could you say the same thing? Yet, that's how a faithful Christian should live.

How are you doing in those areas?

Make me faithful, Lord. I want to serve you all my days. Amen.

THEME: COMMITMENT

You Can't Serve Two Masters

No servant can serve two masters at the same time. You will hate one of them and love the other. Or you will be faithful to one and dislike the other. You can't serve God and Money at the same time.

LUKE 16:13

"Soccer practice," Dan yelled. He whizzed into the house, got on his uniform, and sped for the car. "Come on, Mom."

Mom got into the car, started it, and drove away in silence. After a while, she said, "Don't you think soccer is becoming a little much?"

"Waddaya mean?" Dan answered.

"You talk soccer. You read soccer. You play soccer. You dream soccer. Where does the Lord fit into this, Dan?"

Dan was stumped. He'd never thought about how the Lord fit into anything. But he should. Some of us try to serve two masters: Jesus, and something else. Money. Sports. Books. Friends. Whatever.

But you can't do it. One will win out over the other. Who's winning in your life?

I really love playing _____, Father. Help me to keep it in its place, so I can serve you while I'm doing it. Amen.

THEME: COMMITMENT

Putting the Lord First

I'm saying those things for your own good. I'm not trying to hold you back. I want you to be free to live in a way that is right. I want you to give yourselves completely to the Lord.

1 CORINTHIANS 7:35

Many people resist the idea of putting Jesus first. They think he'll take all the good things away from them.

But what really happens when we put Jesus first? Often, he gives us the things we want right back and says, "Keep it all in perspective. Serve me, and I'll give you the desires of your heart."

Jesus isn't a killjoy. He doesn't want to take away things we enjoy and love. He only wants to fill our lives with the real blessings. What are they? Character. Goodness. Friendship. Sacrifice. Faith. Love. Sharing.

When we put him first, we get not only him, but everything else, too.

I want to be a kid with character, Jesus. Mold me like you and help me to pray every day. Amen.

THEME: COMMITMENT

Not With All His Heart

Amaziah did what was right in the eyes of the LORD. But he didn't do it with all his heart.

2 CHRONICLES 25:2

Have you ever had your coach or music teacher say, "You're not doing it with all your heart!"

It's a sad testimony. When people don't do something with "all their heart," they hold back. They mess around. They fudge. They're not really into it like they should be.

But what's the worst thing that could ever be said about someone? Maybe this: "He did what was right. But he never did it with all his heart." He just wasn't completely there.

That was Amaziah and many other people of Israel. It could be you or me, too.

Are you living this Christian life with all your heart?

I know sometimes I don't serve you with all my heart, Lord. Change me and make me want to serve you wholeheartedly. Amen.

THEME: COMMITMENT

Turning Away

As Solomon grew older, his wives turned his heart toward other gods. He didn't follow the LORD his God with all his heart. So he wasn't like his father David.

1 KINGS 11:4

This is one of the saddest verses in the Bible. King Solomon started off with one of the best careers in Israel's history. He was the wisest man in the land. He built great works. He had a fine army. People from all over the world came by just to listen to him.

But he did something gravely wrong. He married women who weren't believers in God. When he got old, those women turned him from God to their gods.

Do you have people in your life who try to turn you from your faith? It could be a friend, a teacher, a relative, a parent, a sister, or a brother. Beware. Such people are dangerous. Avoid them if you can, and keep your faith pure.

I love my friend _____, Father, but sometimes he says nasty things about you. Help me to speak the truth to him in love. In Jesus' name, amen.

God Wants You!

The LORD looks out over the whole earth. He gives strength to those who commit their lives completely to him.
2 CHRONICLES 16:9

Did you know God is looking for devoted believers? He's always out there, cruising around the planet, looking for people who will trust and love him.

What does he do when he finds them? He gives them strength, wisdom, hope, and love. Why? So they can succeed at building his kingdom.

God's looking right now. Maybe his eyes are on your heart. What does he see? A heart cluttered up with all sorts of fancies and desires? A heart that wants money or sports accolades? Or a heart that wants him?

The heart that wants him often gets everything else thrown in!

I want so many things in life, Master. But one thing counts, and that one thing is you. Help me focus on you today. Amen.

THEME: COMMITMENT

Definition of a Disciple

Jesus spoke to the Jews who had believed him. "If you obey my teaching," he said, "you are really my disciples. Then you will know the truth. And the truth will set you free."

JOHN 8:31–32

What is a disciple?

The Greek word means "learner" or "understudy." A disciple was one who learned from a teacher or leader by being with him.

Jesus took the definition a little further. It wasn't enough to learn. You also had to obey.

But what was the payoff? If you obeyed, you would know the truth. And the truth would make you free.

That's the wonderful thing about being a disciple of Jesus. You learn the truth. And once you've learned it, no one can shackle you with lies ever again.

Obeying is hard, Lord. I want to obey, but my heart sometimes doesn't care. Forgive me for that, and help me change. In Jesus, amen.

THEME: DISCIPLESHIP

Hating Everything and Following Him

Those who come to me must hate their fathers and mothers. They must hate their wives and children. They must hate their brothers and sisters. And they must hate even their own lives.

LUKE 14:26

This is one of those "hard" verses you find in the Bible every now and then. The question is, how could Jesus tell us to hate such people? Aren't we to love? Aren't we to honor our mothers and fathers?

What Jesus meant was that in comparison to how much you must love him, everything else will look like hatred. How so? When you love Jesus, you speak truth. Even to Mom and Dad. Even when they don't want to hear it. When you love Jesus, you'll go anywhere in the world to serve him. Even if your friends think you're crazy.

Jesus wants disciples. Who are they? People who love him more than anyone else in all of the world.

I love you, Father, but sometimes I love _____ more. Show me the right way to love you and them. Amen.

THEME: DISCIPLESHIP

Taking Up Your Cross

Those who don't carry their cross and follow me can't be my disciples.

LUKE 14:27

Jesus said many times that we must take up a cross to follow him properly. What did he mean? Surely he doesn't want us to go get a cross—a means of Roman execution—and follow him around?

No, Jesus was saying, "If you want to follow me, you must leave your old life behind. You must be willing to die for me. You must die to all the things that once were important to you."

That sounds harsh. Tough. Was he asking too much?

He was asking no more than what he did for us. He died on the cross for us. He gave his life for us. He actually did those things! He's asking us only to be willing to do those things for him.

That's not much to ask for a Lord who has given us everything.

This taking-up-the-cross business is difficult to under-stand, Jesus, but I want to do it. Show me your way for me. Amen.

THEME: DISCIPLESHIP

GiViNG Up EVerything You Have

In the same way, you must give up everything you have. If you don't, you can't be my disciple.

LUKE 14:33

Again, more hard words. But that's the cost of following Christ.

"Give up baseball? Give up my card collection? Give up my Nintendo games? Give up my family?"

Jesus is saying, "You must literally give everything up. Whatever I ask you to do, you must do. That might mean doing some things you don't naturally want to do. Like go to a far country. Or live in the slums. To be my disciple, you have to be ready to move when I tell you. And that means being willing to leave everything else behind."

The amazing thing is that when we give up all for him, he returns all back to us in the next breath.

But first you have to give it up, without expecting he will give it all back.

Today I want to give up _____ for you, Master. I hope you'll give it back to me, but whatever you do, I know it'll be right. In Jesus' name, amen.

THEME: DISCIPLESHIP

Becoming Like Him

Students are not better than their teachers. But all who are completely trained will be like their teachers.

LUKE 6:40

Larry Bird, the famed Boston Celtics forward, is now coach of the Indiana Pacers. He wants to teach his team everything he knows. What is his goal? That they as players become as good as he was—or even better!

That's Jesus' goal for your life, too. He wants to train you. He wants to lead you. He wants to tell you everything he knows about living. In the end, his plan is that you become like him. Not in looks. Not in manners and personality. But in character. He wants you to be good, kind, strong, persevering, faithful, loving, and everything else he is.

Why? Because that was God's goal all along. That's what it means to be created in God's image. We'll be little replicas of him. Then when someone asks what he's like, he can point to you or me and say, "Like him!"

Teach me to be like you, Jesus. Today, help me especially with _____. It's a quality I need in my life right now. Amen.

THEME: DISCIPLESHIP

The Goal of a Disciple

So you must go and make disciples of all nations. Baptize them in the name of the Father and of the Son and of the Holy Spirit. Teach them to obey everything I have commanded you.

MATTHEW 28:19–20

If you're a disciple, what is your purpose in life?

To make other disciples. To help other Christians become as godly and committed as you are.

Is it that simple? Yes, that's God's whole plan. Making disciples of everyone on our planet.

How can you do that? By leading a friend to Christ and then teaching her everything you know. Spend time with her. Be with her. Write her notes and letters. Give her your encouragements.

As you do that, you make a disciple. And God will be mightily pleased.

I'd like to make a disciple of _____, Lord. He's a good friend, and I hope you'll work in his heart today. In Jesus, amen.

THEME: DISCIPLESHIP

The Reward of a Disciple

Suppose someone gives even a cup of cold water to a little one who follows me. What I'm about to tell you is true. That one will certainly be rewarded.

MATTHEW 10:42

Did you know God likes giving rewards?

Yes, he promises all through Scripture to reward those who follow him. In this passage, a simple thing like giving water to a child is enough to get a reward. God will give us great blessings for little acts of obedience. What can you do to gain rewards in God's eyes?

Obey your parents.

Do your best in school and study.

Help hurting or needy people.

Give some of your money to God's work.

Worship him daily.

God's promise is sure. When we obey, he rewards. It's that simple.

Teach me to obey you in everything, Father. Teach me to please you with my words and deeds. Amen.

THEME: DISCIPLESHIP

Stand Firm!

Like a good soldier of Christ Jesus, share in the hard times with us.

2 TIMOTHY 2:3

The Bible often refers to us as being soldiers. We're to be tough, like soldiers. We're to keep going no matter how tired, like soldiers. We're to face the enemy with courage, like soldiers.

Above all, a soldier stands firm. He does not give in to the temptation to run in hard times. He endures.

Perhaps the most honored characteristic of a saint in the Bible is endurance. People who stick with it are blessed. People who "hang in there" even when they feel hung are God's beloved. People who refuse to run when everyone else is giving up win God's attention and commendation.

Where are you in the battle? Are you running? Or have you given up?

I want to be a soldier in your army, Jesus. Teach me to endure and to stand firm.
Amen.

THEME: PERSEVERANCE

You Will Rule!

If we died with him, we will also live with him. If we don't give up, we will also rule with him.

2 TIMOTHY 2:11–12

"It's no use, I give up," Emily cried. The doll's arm just wouldn't go back into the slot.

Her mother said, "Let me see it." For a minute or two she worked on it. Suddenly she had it. The arm stuck.

"You did it!" Emily said.

"When you refuse to give up, you often win in the end," her mother answered.

It's true. The one who stays on his feet wins the game. The one who keeps kicking the ball becomes the champion. The one who doesn't give in to anything ends up a contender.

That's the Christian life. Step by step. Staying on your feet. Hanging in there even when all seems to be lost. God promises in the end we will win. So don't give up.

Today I felt like giving up, Lord. Help me to hang in there even when I'm tired. Amen.

THEME: PERSEVERANCE

Blessing Is Just Around the Corner

As you know, we think that people who don't give up are blessed. You have heard that Job was patient. And you have seen what the Lord finally did for him. The Lord is full of tender mercy and loving concern.

JAMES 5:11

Job was a man just like most of us. He faced one of the hardest trials in all of life. He lost his possessions. He lost his kids. He lost his health. But he didn't give up his faith. Instead, he repeatedly called on God to come down and tell him what he'd done wrong! He didn't lose faith. His faith was strengthened by his trial.

What happens to you when bad things happen?

You lose an important game.

You get a C on a big test.

You lose out on a position on the student council.

Do you give up? Do you scream and cry and groan? Try enduring. God blesses that one.

I so wanted to win this week at _____. But I didn't. Help me to accept the loss, and help me to do better next time. In Jesus, amen.

THEME: PERSEVERANCE

Putting Up With Hard Things

Suppose a person suffers pain unfairly because he wants to obey God. That is worthy of praise. But suppose you receive a beating for doing wrong, and you put up with it. Will anyone honor you for that? Of course not.

1 PETER 2:19–20

There are two kinds of bad things in life that we have to put up with: (1) Things that happen to us even though we did the right thing, and (2) Things that happen to us because we did the wrong thing.

Which one of these deserves praise?

Number one, of course. But in our day, victim's rights are a big thing. Even victims who did wrong things. Did you hear about the basketball player who beat up his coach and then screamed about being kicked out the league?

When you do something wrong, accept your punishment. Don't scream or cry. Then go do what's right, and prove you really aren't the kind of person who does wrong things to begin with!

Thank you, Lord, for helping me to accept the consequences when I've done wrong. Let me do right next time. Amen.

THEME: PERSEVERANCE

Look at the Truth and Then Do It

But suppose you take a good look at the perfect law that gives freedom. You keep looking at it. You don't forget what you've heard, but you do what the law says. Then you will be blessed in what you do.

JAMES 1:25

The boy sat in the principal's office. "Do you know the eighth commandment in the Bible?" the principal asked.

Since this was a private school that taught the Bible, the boy knew it. He'd memorized it in first grade. "Yes, it says, 'Do not steal.'"

"Then why did you steal the money from the class treasury?"

"I don't know," the boy said. "I just wanted it."

"And you didn't care what the law says?"

"I guess not."

How many people read the Bible but don't do what it says? It's the person who reads it and obeys it whom God blesses. Are you reading *and* obeying?

Teach me to care about your laws, Father, and help me never to forget them in school. In Jesus' name, amen.

THEME: PERSEVERANCE

Put Up or Shut Up!

We work hard with our own hands. When others call down a curse on us, we bless them. When we are attacked, we put up with it. When others say bad things about us, we answer kindly.

1 CORINTHIANS 4:12–13

The apostle Paul went through nearly everything. Beatings. Whippings. Banishments. Shipwrecks. Lost at sea. Stonings. Death.

But how did he respond to the people who did those things to him? He encouraged them to become Christians. He spoke to them kindly. He forgave them. He helped them when they hurt.

Look at the above Scripture. See what Paul did: Curse us, we bless. Attack us, we stand firm. Say bad things about us, we answer kindly.

What do you do when people mistreat you? It doesn't mean becoming a doormat. No, it means opening the door for them to life in Christ. That's not a doormat; that's a disciple.

A while ago, _____ mistreated me, Jesus. Help me to love them and forgive them the way you would. Amen.

THEME: PERSEVERANCE

Be Faithful, Be Blessed

You need to be faithful. Then you will do what God wants. You will receive what he has promised.

HEBREWS 10:36

Faithfulness is simple: it's doing what God wants, even when we don't want to.

That's hard. Sometimes, anyway. Are you faithful

in doing what your mom and dad ask?
in keeping up with your studies?
in telling the truth to your friends?
in sharing your faith with outsiders?
in going to church and worshiping God?

The faithful person is the one God blesses. If you want to be blessed, then be faithful. Then sit back and let God do his thing!

I wasn't faithful in the matter of _____, Lord. Remind me to think better next time and to do what's right. In Jesus' name, amen.

THEME: PERSEVERANCE

Follow Me!

"Come. Follow me," Jesus said. "I will make you fishers of people."

MARK 1:17

Jesus wants us to follow him. But how does that happen? Jesus isn't a person walking around in tennis shoes and jeans. He's invisible. He's a spirit.

Yet, Jesus still leads. One way we can follow him is to obey his Word. Another way is to follow other strong Christians. Mom. Dad. Your pastor. Your teachers. These are all leaders Jesus uses to help you learn about him.

When Jesus told the disciples he would make them fishers of people, they were excited. For the first time in their lives, they had direction. Something to live for.

That's what following Jesus is all about. When we walk with him, he gives our lives meaning. We count for something. He will use us to accomplish great deeds for his kingdom.

The question is: Are you following?

I know my life counts in your eyes, Jesus. Show me how to count even more! Amen.

Follow in His Steps

Christ suffered for you. He left you an example. He expects you to follow in his steps. You too were chosen to suffer.

1 PETER 2:21

Many years ago, Charles Sheldon wrote a novel called *In His Steps*. It was about a church in a small town that decided to follow Jesus closely in their actions and attitudes. Before they did anything, they asked a simple question: What would Jesus do?

Today, we have bracelets with the initials W.W.J.D. It stands for "What would Jesus do?"

Sometimes following in Jesus' steps is as simple as that question. Suppose every time you had to make a decision, you asked, "What would Jesus do?" Would that change your decisions? Would that help you live for him?

Try it today. Next time you face a tough situation, ask, What would Jesus do? Then go do it!

Lord, thanks for reminding me to consider what you would do in my situation. Amen.

THEME: FOLLOWING JESUS

Live a Worthy Life

I am a prisoner because of the Lord. So I am asking you to live a life worthy of what God chose you for.

EPHESIANS 4:1

"Why does God want me?" Alan asked. "I mean, I'm nobody."

"But God will make you somebody," his youth leader said. "In fact, he's already made you somebody by dying for you."

"But what can I do for him? He already has everything."

"The one thing God doesn't have, which he desires, is our hearts. You can give him your heart."

That's a good start. When we give God our hearts, we're saying, "You lead me. You're in charge. I will follow you."

Paul says here that we should live lives that are worthy of God. What does that mean? Simply living in a way that honors who Jesus is. When we do that, he is pleased.

Once again, Lord, I give you my heart. I know I've done it before, but it's a good reminder. Now lead me to live for you with all my heart. Amen.

THEME: FOLLOWING JESUS

Imitate Their Faith

Remember your leaders. They spoke God's word to you. Think about the results of their way of life. Copy their faith.
HEBREWS 13:7

Every day, Cara's teacher, Miss Jenkins, prayed for the class. She had a little box of three-by-five cards that she wrote prayer requests on. Then she prayed—in class, and on her own time.

Cara studied her teacher. She liked the way Miss Jenkins prayed. It was always fresh, real, like she was truly talking to someone. Plus, she never forgot a prayer request. That box was the key. It helped Miss Jenkins remember who and what to pray for.

One day Cara decided to make her own box. She used it for her prayer time, and it became very important to her. When she grew up, she showed the kids in her own classes the same thing.

That's how we copy the faith of our leaders. By imitating the things they do. It's not hard. It's just a matter of watching, thinking, and applying what we've learned.

_____ at church is a good leader, Father. Help me copy her example. In Jesus' name, amen.

THEME: FOLLOWING JESUS

Live in Him

You received Christ Jesus as Lord. So keep on living in him.

COLOSSIANS 2:6

What does it mean to live in Jesus? We can't go inside him, can we, like a microbe? So what did Paul mean?

To live in Jesus means living in a world where he is your companion. Wherever you are, he is there. Whatever you're doing, he's a part. To live in Jesus is to live as if he's part of everything you do.

What would happen if we really did that? Some things would change, wouldn't they? We wouldn't listen to certain kinds of music, if we knew Jesus was there listening too, would we? We wouldn't go to certain types of movies. Or watch certain programs on TV. Or say certain things to our friends and schoolmates.

If Jesus is with us all the time, our lives have to be different. We recognize he's there. So we don't do the things that make him ashamed.

I know you're always there, Jesus. Help me to remember you're there when I talk to my friends. Sometimes I say things I shouldn't. In Jesus' name, amen.

THEME: FOLLOWING JESUS

Led by the Spirit

But if you are led by the Spirit, you are not under the authority of the law.

GALATIANS 5:18

There are two ways God leads people: by his laws and by his Spirit. Which is better?

Obviously, by his Spirit. The Spirit is a friend. He understands a situation. Hard rules and laws only make us feel guilty. But the Spirit leads naturally. He motivates us. He encourages us. He's the friend deep down inside our hearts.

Do you ever feel the Spirit's leading? The main way he leads is by his Word. But sometimes he speaks to our hearts. It's like a "still, small voice" in our souls. Listen for him today. He'll speak. And then you'll have an opportunity to obey, and please God.

Teach me to listen for the Spirit's leading, Lord, so that I can please you all day long. In Jesus, amen.

THEME: FOLLOWING JESUS

He Will Lead us to Springs of Water

The Lamb, who is at the center of the area around the throne, will be their shepherd. He will lead them to springs of living water. And God will wipe away every tear from their eyes.

REVELATION 7:17

Do you know that one day you will be with Jesus forever? He'll be there. Next to you. Walking along. Talking. Conversing. Being a friend. And maybe he'll say, "Hey, would you like to taste the best water since the creation of time?"

You think that sounds interesting. "Sure."

And he'll lead you to a stream. The water is pure. Crystal clear. Cold. Delicious. And you know what happens when you drink it? You live. You move up to a higher level of life where joy, love, friendship, goodness, and peace are all real and beautiful.

Do you want to drink that water? Then follow him now. He'll get you there.

Let me taste that living water now, Father. I want to be refreshed. In Jesus' name, amen.

THEME: FOLLOWING JESUS

Entertaining Angels

Don't forget to welcome strangers. By doing that, some people have welcomed angels without knowing it.

Angels are everywhere. Sometimes they even come to our house or church. They come as strangers, normal people like you and me. But they're angels in disguise.

How would you know an angel if you saw one? Depending on what form the angel appeared in, it could happen many different ways. But the point of this verse is that there are angels among us. We don't know all their powers, but one is to appear as normal human beings.

How would you like to entertain an angel? You'd probably never know. He'd just seem like an ordinary stranger in need. The one thing you can be sure of: they're there, and they're watching us. They are around us, protecting, helping, encouraging. Watch out! That person next to you at the ballpark could be an angel—studying you to see how a Christian behaves himself!

I don't know if I've ever entertained an angel, Lord. But I hope I'll live like there's one at my door every day. Amen.

THEME: ANGELS

Angels Study Us—But Why?

He wanted the rulers and authorities in the heavenly world to come to know his great wisdom. The church would make it known to them.

EPHESIANS 3:10

Angels watch and study us. Why? To learn God's great wisdom.

You see, angels are either good or bad. They can't be saved. If they aligned themselves with Satan, they're lost. They're fighting God right now. But they know their time is short.

Good angels stuck with God. But in many ways, they weren't sure why. Satan had told them God was a goof. He couldn't be trusted. He didn't know how to run things.

So God came up with a plan. He created the world and the universe to be a means to show off his goodness, wisdom, love, and grace. Now angels study us to learn about those things.

Just think: one might be watching you now. You're not doing anything wrong, are you?

I like the idea of angels studying me, Jesus. Help me to do right so they'll have something good to report! Amen.

THEME: ANGELS

Angels Are Powerful

The angel reached his hand out to destroy Jerusalem. But the LORD was very sad because of the plague.... He said, "That is enough! Do not kill any more people."

2 SAMUEL 24:16

Angels possess tremendous power. In this passage, King David did something wrong. God punished him with a plague on his people. The plague was carried out by an angel.

Notice that: one angel. In this plague, 70,000 people died. Now that's immense power.

In another text, God sent an angel to deliver Jerusalem from a king who attacked them. That angel killed 185,000 soldiers in one night.

Hey, don't mess with angels. They have the real stuff. But remember: they're on your side!

Thank you, Lord, for sending your angels to protect us. I'm glad they're on our side. Amen.

THEME: ANGELS

Angel Food Cake

Then he lay down under the tree. And he fell asleep. Suddenly an angel touched him. The angel said, "Get up and eat." Elijah looked around. Near his head he saw a flat cake of bread.

1 KINGS 19:5–6

Angels are not only powerful; they minister to people in need.

In this passage, Elijah had run from Jezebel, King Ahab's evil wife. He was so tired, he fell asleep under a tree. While he was sleeping, this angel prepared him some food. Later on, after another meal of this "angel food cake," Elijah wouldn't eat for forty days. He wasn't fasting, though. No, that angel cake strengthened him so much he didn't need any more food.

You never know when an angel will appear. One of their primary duties is to help God's people when they're in need. So be ready. Next time you're in need, you might get a helping of angel food cake.

You tell us constantly not to worry about things, Lord, and I'm trying. But help me to remember that your protecting angels are everywhere. In Jesus, amen.

THEME: ANGELS

Messengers of God

But as Joseph was thinking about this, an angel of the Lord appeared to him in a dream. The angel said, "Joseph, son of David, don't be afraid to take Mary home as your wife. The baby inside her is from the Holy Spirit."

MATTHEW 1:20

Another way angels minister is to bring messages. The angel Gabriel came to the virgin Mary in Luke 1 and told her she would have Jesus. That same angel has appeared in other times and other places. In each case, he brought a message from God.

Normally, God doesn't often send angels with messages. His Word covers most everything. But every now and then, there are stories of someone meeting an angel. It happens. They are God's messengers. And they never stutter.

Just as angels are your messengers to us, help me, Father, to be a messenger for you. In Jesus' name, amen.

Pick the Locks

But during the night an angel of the Lord came. He opened the prison doors and brought the apostles out.

ACTS 5:19

Did you know that angels can even pick locks? Probably not like modern criminals and spies. They don't need any equipment. They probably just speak a word and the lock opens.

In the above passage, an angel delivers Peter and John from prison. The Pharisees had locked them up with the idea of possibly executing them. But God intervened. He sent an angel to set them free.

There are modern stories of people being released from prisons, too. Some believe angels have helped Christians the world over. It's really quite believable. If angels watch over us and protect us, surely they can do something as simple as opening a prison door.

In fact, when God chooses to act, no door will keep him out.

Thank you, Lord, for sending your angels to watch over and protect me. Amen.

THEME: ANGELS

Service Is the Name of the Game

All angels are spirits who serve. God sends them to serve those who will receive salvation.

HEBREWS 1:14

The main thing angels do is serve. They serve God. They do whatever he asks. And they do it with joy. Angels are the ultimate good guys. They do only what God wants, nothing more, nothing less. They live to serve God.

We can take a lesson from them. Just as angels serve wholeheartedly, completely, and perfectly, so we ought to serve the same way. If an angel were to scrub the streets of New York City, he would do it with the same joy that Gabriel had when he told Mary she would be the mother of Jesus. If an angel were ordered to wash dishes, he would probably whistle as he worked.

Why? Because serving God is the greatest pleasure. When you know you're serving him, no task is too small. No job is useless. Everything in life has value.

Help me to serve you like your angels do, Master, with joy and a skip in my step. Amen.

THEME: ANGELS

Love God With All ...

Love the Lord your God with all your heart and with all your soul. Love him with all your mind.

MATTHEW 22:37

How does God want us to love him? Jesus spells out three ways in this verse.

1. Love him with all your heart. That's with the core of your being. The deepest parts of yourself. Love him with your motives and your secrets. Hold nothing back.

2. Love him with all your soul. That's with your personality. Bring your own unique ways of loving him to him. Show him all the crazy ways you can do it. Get into it.

3. Love him with all your mind. Study him. Find out who he is. Learn his Word. Think. God wants us to be mature, thinking people. He wants us to love him with our minds. No question or doubt is beyond bringing to him.

When you love God like that, you really love him.

Teach me to love you, Lord, with all my soul, heart, mind, and might. That way I know I'll do it right. Amen.

THEME: LOVING GOD

Those Terrible Neighbors

Love your neighbor as you love yourself.

MATTHEW 22:39

One of the best ways to love God is to love his people. When we love people, we are actually loving God. Why? Because he put them there. He made them. They're in his image.

How can we love his people?

By helping an old lady clean her house.
By praying for the need of a friend.
By letting someone else go first.
By befriending the new kid in town.
By giving a dollar to a needy person.

There are a million ways. The important thing is that you do them.

Give me an opportunity today, Jesus, to serve you. Let me do it with happiness, too, the way that pleases you. Amen.

THEME: LOVING GOD

The Liar

Suppose someone says, "I know him." But suppose that person does not do what God commands. Then that person is a liar and is not telling the truth.

1 JOHN 2:4

How do you know if a person really is a Christian? By whether they obey God's Word.

John says here that people who claim to know God but don't obey his commands are liars.

Is that harsh? Not at all. There are many impostors out there. Many fakes. They can easily suck us into their games. We need to beware.

When a person says he loves God, there has to be evidence in his life. He will not commit outright sin. Or if he does, he'll repent and change his ways. People who disobey God without looking back are fakes. Avoid them.

I don't want to be a fake Christian, Lord. Teach me to do things not only with my body, but with my heart as well. Amen.

THEME: LOVING GOD

Don't Love the World

Do not love the world or anything in it. If you love the world, love for the Father is not in you.

1 JOHN 2:15

"Please, please, please give me Nintendo for Christmas!" Carl said. He begged over and over. Should his parents give him Nintendo?

Let's take a look at Carl's room. All kinds of guns, games, sports equipment, and toys spilled out of his closet and filled every shelf. When Carl went to the store with his mom, he wanted everything he saw. And sometimes he threw a fit if he didn't get it.

That's a kid who loves the world. His eyes are on the things the world produces. He wants what the world can give.

A true Christian doesn't worry about the world. If he gets Nintendo or not, he knows he'll survive. His first love is Jesus.

What do you love the most?

I know I love some things this world makes, Jesus. Help me to keep it all in proportion. Help me to love you first. Amen.

THEME: LOVING GOD

The Real Thing

Here is how you can tell the difference between the children of God and the children of the devil. Those who don't do what is right do not belong to God. Those who don't love their brothers do not belong to him either.

1 JOHN 3:10

How do you know who's the real thing in God's kingdom? How do you know if a person is a real Christian? By whether they do what's right.

That's what John says.

Terri said, "I think she's a Christian. But she talks so mean sometimes. I hear her and I feel bad."

"Maybe we need to tell her to stop that," Claire answered.

"I did," Terri answered. "And then she turned on me."

Christians are sinners. Some people are more mature than others. But real Christians should want to do what's right. That's how they love God—by doing what he wants.

Help me to do what is right, dear Lord, and help me to love the people around me, as you love me. Amen.

THEME: LOVING GOD

Obeying Is Not Hard

Here is what it means to love God. It means that we obey his commands. And his commands are not hard to obey.

1 JOHN 5:3

The way we love God is by obeying him. Some say, "That's hard." But in most of the situations of life, obeying God is not hard. It's simply a matter of knowing what his Word says and then doing it.

A boy looked in a parakeet cage. The bird was huddled in a corner, eyeing him. The boy's friend was out of the room.

Suddenly, the boy pulled a pen out of his pocket and poked it into the cage. He was about to poke the bird, when the still, small voice spoke in his head: "Is that the right way to treat this bird, one of God's creatures?"

For a moment, the boy hung his head. Then he put the pencil back in his pocket.

Obeying God can be as easy and simple as that. It's a matter of choice.

I was tempted today, Lord, about _____. But I did the right thing, and I'm happy. Amen.

Hating Your Brothers

Those who say they love God but in fact hate a brother are liars. They don't love a brother, whom they have seen. So they can't love God, whom they have not seen.

1 JOHN 4:20

"I hate him! He's the worst brother on earth!" Candace screeched.

Dad shook his head. "Don't talk that way, honey."

"But I do. He's such a nerd."

"God says if you hate your brother, you're a liar."

Candace frowned. "What do you mean?"

Dad explained, "If you don't love your brother, who is right in front of you, how can you love God, whom you can't see?"

Candace thought about it. Finally, she said, "I'm sorry. I didn't mean it. I want to love God. And I want to try to love my brother too."

Hatred is an evil thing. God says that to hate your brothers and sisters is a sign you're not really one of his children.

So stop hating and start loving. It's a lot more fun.

Sometimes I hate my siblings, Lord. Help me to love them even when they bother me. Amen.

THEME: LOVING GOD

Loving Like Jesus Loved

I give you a new command. Love one another. You must love one another just as I have loved you. If you love one another, everyone will know you are my disciples.

JOHN 13:34–35

Jesus gave us only a few commands in Scripture. The foremost is this one: Love one another as he loved us.

How did Jesus love us? Think about it. He did a number of things that make his love for us unique and wonderful.

1. He served. Wherever he went, he was willing to help and serve others.
2. He spoke the truth. Even when others didn't like it. Even when they got mad and threatened him.
3. He sacrificed his life. The biggie. Jesus went to the cross for all of us.

That's some love, isn't it? And that's how Jesus wants us to love each other. Can you begin doing that today?

Lord, help me to love others by serving them and telling them the truth. Thank you for your great love. Amen.

THEME: LOVING OTHERS

Love Comes from God

Dear friends, let us love one another, because love comes from God. Everyone who loves has been born again because of what God has done.

1 JOHN 4:7

"God is love," John said in the letter we know as 1 John. It's one of God's chief traits. If we are connected to God, then we should see him working in us and through us. One of the ways he will use us is to love others.

Have you ever heard one of these statements?

"I can't love her. She hurt me too much."

"I can't stand him. He messes up everything."

"I'll never forgive him for what he did. Never!"

Christians might speak such words, but they should also repent. God loves everyone, even his enemies. That's the way we should love, too.

_____ *is my enemy, Jesus. You know her and her heart. Help me to care for her the way you would. Amen.*

What Is Love Like?

Love is patient. Love is kind. It does not want what belongs to others. It does not brag. It is not proud.

1 CORINTHIANS 13:4

Wow! What a list. Every one of those things is tough to do.

Patience? "If you had my little brother, you'd go crazy."

Kind? "You don't know the kids at school. Some of them are real mean."

Bragging? "But I just got a good grade on a hard test. Can't I tell anyone about it?"

Pride? "It's my new bike. It goes fast. Why shouldn't I feel good about it?"

Those are all good arguments. But love chooses the other way in each case. It stays patient with little brothers, even when they push it. It's kind, like the Good Samaritan. It doesn't brag (though it might enjoy having good grades). And it's not proud.

That's a hard list to live. But with the Holy Spirit in us, all things are possible.

Lord, help me to choose to love, even when it's hard. Amen.

THEME: LOVING OTHERS

Enemies!

You have heard that it was said, "Love your neighbor. Hate your enemy." But here is what I tell you. Love your enemies. Pray for those who hurt you.

MATTHEW 5:43–44

Dale and Mark stood opposite one another. "You come a step closer, I'll punch you!" Mark said.

"You stole my baseball cards!" Dale yelled. "Give them back."

"I didn't steal them."

"Larry told me you did."

"Then I'll fight him, too."

Both boys eyed one another. A second later, a teacher arrived. He made both boys shake hands, but Dale was still angry. What should he do?

Jesus has two words: Love Mark and pray for him. That gives God some room to work. Maybe through the Lord's help, the problem will be worked out. But even if nothing happens, Dale still needs to love and pray.

_____ is difficult to love, Father. Show me something about him that will make it easier, I pray. In Jesus, amen.

THEME: LOVING OTHERS

More Marks of Love

[Love] is not rude. It does not look out for its own interests. It does not easily become angry. It does not keep track of other people's wrongs. Love is not happy with evil. But it is full of joy when the truth is spoken.

1 CORINTHIANS 13:5–6

Anna stood in the middle of her room, her face red. "You did it again!"

"What did I do this time?" her sister Olivia asked.

"You took my CD."

"I did not!"

Anna held the CD up. "I found this in your room."

Olivia hung her head. "I'm sorry."

"Sorry doesn't make it anymore!" Anna yelled. "This is the fourth time you've done it. And before that you took my books without asking. And before that . . ."

What is Anna doing here? She is keeping a record of her sister's wrongs. Love doesn't do that. It forgives each one as they're done. And then forgets about it.

Do you forgive like that?

Sometimes my siblings and I fight, Lord. I bring up all the old wrongs, and I know that's wrong. Help me to fight fair and forgive, too. Amen.

THEME: LOVING OTHERS

What Love Always Does

[Love] always protects. It always trusts. It always hopes. It never gives up. Love never fails.

1 CORINTHIANS 13:7–8

"I hope you flunk!" Charles shouted.

"And I hope you get kicked out of the class," Don answered.

The argument went back and forth. Soon they were both saying bad things about each other's families, mothers, and everyone else. When a teacher intervened, the argument didn't stop. The bad thing is that both Charles and Don went to the same church. They were both Christians.

What happens when we Christians fail to love each other? The world notices. It says, "Even Christians hate each other! So what's so bad about the rest of us?"

It shouldn't be that way. Love protects its friends and even its enemies. It trusts in God and other Christians. And it hopes the best for them.

How are you loving those around you today?

There are some kids at church that I just don't like, Jesus. I know that's wrong thinking, so help me to love them. Amen.

THEME: LOVING OTHERS

The Devotion of Love

Love must be honest and true. Hate what is evil. Hold on to what is good. Love each other deeply. Honor others more than yourselves.

ROMANS 12:9–10

Here are more words about loving that are beautiful but hard. Yet, imagine what your life might be like if you loved like that.

You'd be "honest and true." People would trust you. They'd look up to you. They'd give you responsibilities and privileges.

You'd "hate what is evil." You'd stand on the side of the underdog and the hurting.

You'd "hold on to what is good." You'd never let good things go. And you'd share them with others.

You'd "love deeply." That's from the heart. People would know you really care.

You'd "honor others." You'd let them shine and look good.

Imagine if others did that for you! Then do it for them, and see what happens.

I'd like to honor _____, Jesus. Show me a good way to do it that will be fun and loving. Amen.

THEME: LOVING OTHERS

Love by Obeying

Children, obey your parents as believers in the Lord. Obey them because it's the right thing to do.

EPHESIANS 6:1

Hannah was playing in the backyard when her dad cried out. "Stop and stand very still, Hannah."

The girl was about to say something, but she obeyed.

Her father strode slowly toward her. "Now don't move as I shout," he said. He suddenly waved his arms and yelled. Hannah almost jumped. But in front of her, something rattled and then slithered through the grass.

A rattlesnake!

Hugging her, Hannah's dad said, "It's a good thing you know how to obey, honey. That snake was about to bite you."

Most of the time perfect obedience isn't a matter of life and death. But if you're wise, you'll learn to obey your parents. They serve under God to raise you in the faith and help you walk with him.

I know I should obey my parents, Father, but it's hard sometimes. Help me to do it with a right attitude. Amen.

THEME: LOVING YOUR FAMILY

The Commandment with a Promise

Scripture says, "Honor your father and mother." That is the first commandment that has a promise. "Then things will go well with you. You will have a long time on the earth."

EPHESIANS 6:2–3

Only one of the Ten Commandments has a promise attached to it. Do you know what one it is?

The fifth: "Honor your father and mother." What's the promise? Paul lays it out in the passage above. "Things will go well with you. You'll live a long time."

Those are two heavy promises, aren't they? Kids who fight and defy their parents often grow up with big problems in life. They can't get along. They can't keep a job. Sometimes they become criminals and die young.

Don't let that happen to you. Honor Mom and Dad now and all will be well.

I want to live a long time, but I want to also live it for you, Lord. In Jesus, amen.

THEME: LOVING YOUR FAMILY

Suffering in the Home

When you hope, be joyful. When you suffer, be patient. When you pray, be faithful.

ROMANS 12:12

Not all homes are healthy. Some parents are neglectful, violent, or abusive. The news reports cases of abuse almost every day.

How should young Christians deal with such circumstances? By loving their parents like Paul says. "When you suffer, be patient. When you pray, be faithful." How does that work when you're hurting?

Be patient. Trust the Lord. Expect him to help. You may be surprised at what he does. Eventually, your patience will pay off.

Be faithful when you pray. That means, don't disobey God. Don't pray that Dad will stop drinking and then be disobedient and nasty to him. Don't pray that Mom will stop slapping you and then sass her to her face.

Family problems don't have easy solutions. But when God is in charge, you can be sure he'll do something to help.

I pray for my mom and dad, Lord. They're having a hard time right now and they need your help. Amen.

THEME: LOVING YOUR FAMILY

Make Your Home a Welcoming Place

Share with God's people who are in need. Welcome others into your homes.

ROMANS 12:13

"Jon's here," Mrs. Andrews called to Russ.

"Hey," Jon said, "got anything good to eat, Mrs. Andrews?"

"I sure do!" Mrs. Andrews said. "Come on in." She led Russ and Jon into the kitchen, where they had some brownies and milk.

"Thanks, Mrs. Andrews," said Jon. "You've always got good stuff."

Russ felt good that Jon liked coming over. His mother always helped his friends feel welcome.

Work to make your home a welcoming place. Greet your guests with a smile. Serve snacks. Be pleasant and courteous. Your house will become a magnet, and you'll never lack for friends.

Lord, thanks for everything my parents do to make my house a home. Help me also to welcome others when they come to visit. Amen.

THEME: LOVING YOUR FAMILY

When People in Your Family Hurt You

Bless those who hurt you. Bless them, and do not call down curses on them.

ROMANS 12:14

Lisa's older brother was angry again. He cursed and yelled at Lisa's mom. When Lisa tried to stop him, he slammed her into a wall. Then he stomped out of the house, yelling that he'd burn the place down.

It happens. Not all homes are Christian homes. What would you recommend that Lisa do in this situation?

If her brother is abusive, it's time to suggest he leave. Or get help from a pastor or counselor. For Lisa, blessing her brother instead of cursing him will help. That means being kind, offering to help, and being friendly even if he isn't. He may react with laughter at her goodness, but something will get through.

God can work through Christians who bless those who hurt them.

Let me be kind to both my friends and my enemies, Lord. That way they'll all know I belong to you. Amen.

THEME: LOVING YOUR FAMILY

Put Up With It

Cheer up those who are shy. Help those who are weak. Put up with everyone.

1 THESSALONIANS 5:14

"Wanna see me pick my nose?"

Little Jared was grossing out Valerie's friends again. He was only six, but he sure could be a pain.

Here, Paul has a good word for kids with foolish or obnoxious brothers and sisters. What is his advice? "Put up with them."

Why does he say that? Well, for one thing, they're your family. You can't just get rid of them. And yelling, screaming, and hitting will only make matters worse.

For another thing, you've got to give them time to grow up. Growing up is a long process, and it takes time.

Put up with it, and you'll be amazed how eventually people change.

I want to be patient with _____, Jesus, but it's so hard. Please work in him as you teach me to be patient with him. Amen.

Never Pay Back Evil

Make sure that nobody pays back one wrong act with another. Always try to be kind to each other and to everyone else.

1 THESSALONIANS 5:15

Steve sat in the tree fort with his friend, Aseer. "All right, when he comes up the ladder, we both spit in his face. If he falls off, too bad."

"But he's your brother, Steve," Aseer said.

"He crashed my bike. Isn't that enough?"

"Yeah, but I thought you were a Christian."

"I am."

"Then I don't—"

"Shut up! Just shut up and do what I say."

Steve is plotting revenge on his brother. And that is a sin. What would you do instead, according to Paul's words above?

Help me to be kind to my brothers and sisters, Jesus, even when they do things that hurt me. Amen.

THEME: LOVING YOUR FAMILY

Respect!

We ask you to have respect for the godly leaders who work hard among you. They have authority over you. They correct you.

1 THESSALONIANS 5:12

The Bible does not say much about regular school. But there are some verses that give us some insight as to how God might feel about leaders, including teachers. This verse is one of them. In it, Paul tells us to respect our teachers.

Here are some things you can easily say about many teachers.

1. They work hard. They put in long days and take work home with them. Few teachers consider their work easy.
2. They are dedicated. Many like teaching young people. They want to see them excel and learn well.
3. They care about their kids. They really do.

These are good reasons to respect any teacher.

I pray for my teachers, Lord. They often have a hard time with us, but I hope you'll bless them this week for their hard work. In Jesus' name, amen.

THEME: SCHOOL

Love Your Teachers!

Have a lot of respect for them. Love them because of what they do. Live in peace with each other.

1 Thessalonians 5:13

Paul goes on in this passage to tell us to love our leaders. Why?

Because of what they do, Paul says.

Take a look at the teachers in your school. They have to deal with kids who are unruly. Who talk back. Who make messes. Who hate them. When they find a kid who actually behaves and wants to learn, they're probably amazed.

But why don't you be that kid? Thank your teachers when they help you. Let them know you like them. Tell them you appreciate their hard work.

It may not get you better grades—it shouldn't—but it will please God.

Help me today, Father, to remember to compliment my teacher, _____. I know she works hard and she needs your love. Amen.

Remember Who You Are

Students are not better than their teachers. Servants are not better than their masters.

MATTHEW 10:24

In the movie, *The Lion King*, Mustafa kept telling his son, Simba, to remember who he was. He was the son of a king. He was the end of a long line of great lions. He was ruler over a large piece of land. He had many subjects. But above all, he was a son, a learner at his father's hand.

You are a learner, too. You don't call the shots. You're not the boss in the classroom. You're not the center of attention. You're there to learn. You're there to obey. You're there to get ready for adulthood.

Are you doing those things? If you are, you are on the way toward gaining God's blessing. If you're not— change your ways!

Help me to listen and learn from my teachers, Lord. May I respect them and their knowledge. Amen.

THEME: SCHOOL

Support Your Teacher

Those who are taught the word must share all good things with their teacher.

GALATIANS 6:6

Jesus was always careful to let people know they should support their teachers. This meant paying them money and helping them with their living expenses.

For a young person like you, it means other things. What?

> Saying thank you for help.
>
> Remembering a birthday or anniversary. Sending a card.
>
> Bringing a gift at Christmas. Even if the teacher doesn't give you one.
>
> Helping out when asked.
>
> Listening and paying attention.
>
> Not complaining about them to friends.

You can support your teacher in a lot of ways. What one way can you begin with today?

Show me a way to speak kindly to _____. She's a good teacher and deserves a good word. Amen.

THEME: SCHOOL

One Teacher's Attitude

The Teacher was wise. He gave knowledge to people. He put many proverbs to the test. He thought about them carefully. Then he wrote them down in order. He did his best to find just the right words. And what he wrote was honest and true.

ECCLESIASTES 12:9–10

The Bible is full of great teachers. One of the greatest was King Solomon. He was given God's wisdom. He used that wisdom to write several books of Scripture: Proverbs, Song of Songs, and Ecclesiastes. He also used it to teach his people and his son how to live.

Look at what he says was his outlook: (1) He was wise. (2) He imparted his knowledge. (3) He wrote down what he knew was right. (4) He worked at his teaching. (5) He was honest and true.

That's a good description of many teachers. Maybe even your own teacher. Why not let them know you support them today?

Thank you for my teachers, Lord. Please give them strength to do their jobs well. In Jesus, amen.

THEME: SCHOOL

A Teacher's Orders

Those who serve the Lord must not fight. Instead, they must be kind to everyone. They must be able to teach. They must not hold anything against anyone.

2 TIMOTHY 2:24

Let's not forget the teachers themselves. What can you expect of a teacher in your school? Do they have a responsibility to you?

Here, Paul lays out several ideas about how a teacher of God's Word should act. It's good advice for any teacher.

Good teachers should not fight. Teachers who argue nastily and get hotheaded in class are wrong. They are not teaching wisely.

Good teachers should be kind to everyone. No matter what race, color, or religion. No matter how bad the kids are at times.

Good teachers must not hold grudges.

Just think if all teachers were like that! How much would be learned in their classes!

I pray that my teachers will be wise, kind, and forgiving, Lord. We need it. Amen.

THEME: SCHOOL

The Greatest Teacher of All

God is honored because he is so powerful. He has no equal as a teacher.

JOB 36:22

Who is the best teacher of all?

For a Christian, the answer is obvious: God.

Think about it. Just look at Jesus. He spoke words no one ever heard before. He gave us principles and ideas unknown. He shared stories—the Good Samaritan, the Prodigal Son—that are part of our greatest literature. He instructed all kinds of people—the hurting, the wise, the intelligent, the stupid. He didn't hold back truth from anyone.

Above all, Jesus lived out his teachings. He was not a hypocrite, saying one thing and doing another. We can learn much from him. In fact, we can learn nearly everything from him.

What have you learned from him today?

I know some teachers who say one thing and do another, Father. I pray for them, that you would convict them and change them. In Jesus, amen.

THEME: SCHOOL

How Do You Know You Love?

How do we know that we love God's children? We know it when we love God and obey his commands.

1 JOHN 5:2

"But how do I know when I love someone?" Patti asked. "Sometimes I feel love for people. But sometimes I don't."

"Love is not a feeling," her mother explained. "It's an action."

"But what kind of action?"

"When you help others in need, encourage people, give money—then you know you're loving others. Love is doing things for them."

"But what if I don't feel anything? Is it still love?"

Her mother smiled. "Even if you feel nothing, it doesn't matter. Love is acting to help others. It's not just feeling good inside."

"But when you help others, you do feel good inside. Right?"

"Correct."

As Patti discovered here, obedience is what God wants most. When we obey him, we are loving him.

Teach me to love and obey you, Lord, even when I don't feel like it. In Jesus, amen.

THEME: OBEYING GOD

First and Foremost

Children, obey your parents in everything. That pleases the Lord.

COLOSSIANS 3:20

The first way to obey God is to obey your parents.

"But what if they're wrong?" Gene asked.

He was sincere. He knew his dad had a bad temper. Though he coached Gene's team, he sometimes got into trouble. He yelled and cursed. Not many people liked him.

"How do you know if he's wrong?" Gene's teacher, Mr. Martin, asked.

"Well, what if he wants me to do something against the Bible?"

"Then you refuse to do it."

"What if he won't let me go to church?"

"That's a tricky one," Mr. Martin said. "What I'd do is pray and ask God to soften your dad's heart. God can do it."

Few things in life are straight and plain. But if you obey your parents in the things you know are right, the other doubtful things will fall into place.

I know my parents love me, Father. Help me love them by obeying them. In Jesus' name, amen.

THEME: OBEYING GOD

God's Special Treasure

*Now obey me completely. Keep my covenant. If you do,
then out of all of the nations you will be my special treasure.*
EXODUS 19:5

Do you know what God called Israel when they obeyed him? "My special treasure."

But did God only love them when they obeyed?

No, God loves us even when we don't obey him. But he takes pleasure in us when we do obey. Do you see the difference? God's love doesn't change. But his own feelings matter. He feels good when we obey. He feels bad when we don't.

How would it feel to be God's special treasure? We don't have to ask that. Why? Because we *are* his special treasure now.

So what kind of treasure are you today—an obedient one, or a disobedient one?

Thank you, Jesus, that you call me your treasure. Just help me to live up to it. Amen.

THEME: OBEYING GOD

What to Do With a Leader

Obey your leaders. Put yourselves under their authority. They keep watch over you. They know they are accountable to God for everything they do. Obey them so that their work will be a joy. If you make their work a heavy load, it won't do you any good.

HEBREWS 13:17

"I'm not following him," Edward said. "He's an idiot."

"He's a good guy," Brian countered. "Besides, that's just your opinion. When you joined the church group, you agreed to follow."

"But he always wants us to do stupid stuff."

"Like what?"

"I don't know. It's all stupid."

Edward's problem is a common one. You don't like what the leader wants you to do, so you refuse to follow. But that's not what God tells us to do. He says we should obey our leaders. Why? Because he works through them for us.

Lord, I don't always agree with what my leaders at church want us to do, but help me to be gracious and respectful in my attitude toward them. Amen.

THEME: OBEYING GOD

The Government

Remind God's people to obey rulers and authorities. Remind them to be ready to do what is good.

TITUS 3:1

Joe heard his dad complain about taxes again. He decided to say something about it at dinner. "Dad, why are you always complaining about taxes?"

"Do you know how much of our money the government takes each year?" his dad retorted.

"Yes, but aren't we supposed to obey our government? That's what Pastor Dan said."

His dad squinted angrily. "You don't understand. You're just a kid."

"But we have to do right, don't we, Dad?"

"Don't preach at me!"

Taxes are a hot issue for many parents. But the truth is, God wants us to obey our government. Even if we don't like what they say. Why? Because God works through the government to lead us.

Help me to obey the government, Father, even when I don't like their laws. In Jesus, amen.

THEME: OBEYING GOD

God's Word Is God Speaking

Keep an eye on those who don't obey the directions in our letter. Watch them closely. Have nothing to do with them. Then they will feel ashamed.

2 THESSALONIANS 3:14

When Paul wrote the letter to the Thessalonians, he told them to obey his directions. Why? Because Paul believed his letters came from God. He believed his letters were the very words of God himself.

Is that pride? Wasn't Paul being a little uppity about that?

Not if God called him to what he did. Not if God was with him.

God had to use someone. So he used people like Paul to write the Word of God. God didn't dictate the letters, though. Through his Spirit, he used Paul's personality, ideas, and plans to get across his own Word. It's like building a building. You have the blueprint, but the people lay the bricks. God gave Paul the blueprint and Paul laid the bricks.

And we're to obey them!

I know your Word is from you, Jesus, so I trust it. Thank you for giving us such a perfect, complete Bible so we can know what you want us to do. Amen.

THEME: OBEYING GOD

Stay In Jesus' Love

If you obey my commands, you will remain in my love. In the same way, I have obeyed my Father's commands and remain in his love.

JOHN 15:10

Does Jesus' love for us ever change?

No, he is the same, yesterday and today and forever. His love can never change.

Does Jesus ever want to give up on us?

No, he knows the end from the beginning. He knew all the places where we'd flub up. So he's prepared to deal with them.

Then why does Jesus say, "If you obey ... you will remain in my love"? Does that mean if we don't obey, we lose his love?

No, it means if we obey we will sense his presence and his love for us. When we disobey, his love doesn't change. We change. And we cease to sense his love for us.

Do you want to feel loved? Then obey him. In everything. Always.

Let me feel your love in my heart, Father, so I not only know from your Word that you love me, but from my own thoughts. Amen.

THEME: OBEYING GOD

Knowing More Than Your Teachers

I know more than all of my teachers do, because I spend time thinking about your covenant laws.

PSALM 119:99

"How would you like to know more than your teachers?" Mr. Phelps asked in Sunday school.

Laurie thought that would be great. She'd love to be smarter than her teacher.

Mr. Phelps said, "Do you know how that can happen?"

The students shook their heads.

"Spend your time thinking about God's Word," Mr. Phelps said. "See what it says here in Psalm 119:99?" And he read the verse to them.

When you know the Word of God and think about it, or meditate on it, you will gain great knowledge and insight. Even beyond your teachers.

Now wouldn't that be something?

Let me think and meditate on your Word, Lord. I don't just want to know it in my head, but in my heart. Amen.

THEME: WISDOM

The Wisest Man of Them All

God made Solomon very wise. His understanding couldn't even be measured. It was like the sand on the seashore. People can't measure that either.

1 KINGS 4:29

Who was the wisest man ever?

Undoubtedly, Jesus. But he was God incarnate, too. Surely that gave him a great edge.

Among men, though, King Solomon is considered one of the wisest of all time. This verse above tells us how it happened.

But how did it happen?

Look at the verse again. It says "God made Solomon very wise." It was something God did.

Did you know that God can do that in you too? Imagine if you were as wise as Solomon. Then when you spoke, people would listen!

Make me wise like Solomon, Jesus. In your name, amen.

THEME: WISDOM

Get Wisdom

Wisdom is best. So get wisdom. No matter what it costs, get understanding.

PROVERBS 4:7

What things do you most want to get in life?

Money?
Nintendo games?
New roller blades?
Great grades?

Probably most of us wouldn't think of wisdom as the main thing we should want. But the funny thing about wisdom is this: when you get wisdom, it helps you get most of the other things you want out of life.

So get wisdom. What have you gotten today?

Teach me to get wisdom, Lord, like Solomon and all the great people of the Bible. Teach me to love wisdom, too. Amen.

THEME: WISDOM

The Spirit of the Holy Gods

I know a man in your kingdom who has the spirit of the holy gods in him. He has understanding and wisdom and good sense just like the gods.

DANIEL 5:11

Remember Daniel? He was one of the wisest of all God's saints. Notice what this person says about him:

1. He had a "spirit of the holy gods." That means, they believed he was inhabited by deities. (In fact, God worked in him!)
2. He had understanding. That is, he saw beneath the surface of things. He understood what was really inside of people.
3. He had wisdom. Wisdom is the power to solve problems intelligently.
4. He had "good sense." That is, whatever he said to do made sense to others, even though they hadn't seen it.

Would you like that kind of mental capacity? Then study God's Word. That's what Daniel did.

Daniel is a good example for me, Father. May you give me understanding, wisdom, and good sense, too. Amen.

THEME: WISDOM

Meditation on Scripture

Think about what I am saying. The Lord will help you understand what all of it means.

2 TIMOTHY 2:7

One of the most important things for Christians to do is to "meditate" on Scripture. What does that mean?

The Hebrew word for meditation means to "murmur" or to "talk to yourself." Meditation is like thinking or talking to yourself.

For example, think about the words, "The Lord is my shepherd." You could reflect on what a shepherd does. How he takes care of the sheep. How he protects them. And you could think about how you're like a sheep!

That's meditation. When you meditate, you learn something about God, or something about yourself.

Try it. You will learn something new for sure.

Teach me to meditate on your Word, Eternal Father, so I might please you. In Jesus' name, amen.

THEME: WISDOM

God's Plan

He poured his grace on us by giving us great wisdom and understanding. He showed us the mystery of his plan.

EPHESIANS 1:8–9

Did you ever think about all the wisdom you have just from knowing some basic truths from the Bible?

For instance, what are the three great questions of people? They are: Who am I? Where am I going? What am I supposed to do with my life?

Probably every human being has asked those questions many times in his or her life. But you know the answers if you know the Bible.

"I'm a child of God, loved and kept by Jesus."

"I am going to heaven and I will live with Jesus forever."

"Jesus wants me to obey his Word and live for him."

Most people don't know those answers. But they're there for anyone who will seek Jesus. Who can you point in his direction today?

Thanks for answering the three great questions of life for me, Lord. With those answers, I know I can succeed. Amen.

THEME: WISDOM

Hard Hearts

They had not understood about the loaves. They were stubborn.

MARK 6:52

There is a danger in getting too close to the Word of God. Do you know what it is?

The danger is when you do not take the Word to heart and obey it. What happens then?

Your heart is hardened. You become stubborn, like the disciples in the above story. They didn't understand that Jesus could feed everyone anytime anywhere. They refused to believe he was really God. So their hearts were hardened.

That can happen to you. Anytime you come to God's Word and refuse to listen to it, you undergo a little hardening inside. That can build up until you can't hear God's Word at all.

And then what happens? Then he has to discipline you. That isn't fun at all.

Are you listening to and obeying the Word today?

Lord, help me not to be stubborn. Sometimes I am and I need your help to change. In Jesus, amen.

THEME: WISDOM

The Long View

Childish people believe anything. But wise people think about how they live.

PROVERBS 14:15

A father told his son, "If you save that money, you'll have enough for your first year of college."

"But Dad," said the boy, "I've been hoping to get a new bike!"

His dad answered, "You've got to think about the future, son. You have to take a long view of things. Otherwise you'll fail."

Taking the long view is the ability to consider what you'll need in the future. That's why the verse says that "wise people think about how they live."

Are you thinking about your future? Take some time and look at it. God wants you to think not only about today, but to plan for tomorrow.

Let me take the long view, Father. Let me see where I'm going so I'll know how to get there. Amen.

THEME: UNDERSTANDING

Think of What You Know

We also know that the Son of God has come. He has given us understanding. Now we can know the One who is true. And we belong to the One who is true.

1 John 5:20

Jesus came to give us understanding. That is, he wants to give us knowledge of the plan of God. Where is God taking us? What is he doing in human history? Where will it all end?

If you're a reader of the Bible, you know the answers to those questions. God is taking the world to a marvelous conclusion. Jesus will return. Christians will go to be with him forever. We will reign over the universe. At the same time, Jesus will right every wrong and bring in perfect justice for all people.

Next time someone asks, "What's it all about?" you know the answer. It's about Jesus, his kingdom, and his people.

Thank you for letting me in on what you're doing in world history, Jesus. I trust you to get it all done perfectly. Amen.

THEME: UNDERSTANDING

Rules Can Be Good

Be careful to keep them. That will show the nations how wise and understanding you are. They will hear about all of those rules. They'll say, "That great nation certainly has wise and understanding people."

DEUTERONOMY 4:6

Keeping rules is a sign that people care about each other. Without rules, no one would get along. People would hurt each other and not care. Injustice would occur everywhere.

The nation of Israel was a great nation. One reason was because of its law code. It had one of the best in all of history. God had given the Law to them to guide them in every aspect of life.

When we keep the rules, others say, "You're a good, upstanding citizen." And they want to be your friend. Why? Because they know they can trust you.

Are you trustworthy like that?

I don't always like rules, Lord, but they help the world to work better. Help me to obey the rules and become trustworthy. In Jesus' name, amen.

THEME: UNDERSTANDING

How You Show You're Wise

Are any of you wise and understanding? You should show it by living a good life. Wise people aren't proud when they do good works.

JAMES 3:13

How do you prove you're a wise and understanding person? By living a good life.

That's what James says. What happens when a kid says he's a Christian, but he tells lies? Or steals? Or cheats? You tend to think he's not really a Christian.

What happens when a person gets drunk, beats his family, and hates his neighbors? And then goes to church on Sunday? His kids don't believe him.

If you don't want to grow up to be that kind of Dad or Mom, then start living a good life right now. Do good. Do right. Be wise and kind. This will back up your words and show you're the real thing when you claim to be a Christian.

Help me to back up my life by living right, Lord. Amen.

THEME: UNDERSTANDING

How to Get Full

We have been praying for you since the day we heard about you. We have been asking God to fill you with the knowledge of what he wants. We pray that he will give you spiritual wisdom and understanding.

COLOSSIANS 1:9

"You should meet my grandpa," Kerry said. "He's the smartest man I know."

"Why do you think he's so smart?" Lisa asked.

"Because he's always praying that God will fill him with wisdom."

"All he does is pray?"

"He reads the Bible, too. And he studies it. And lots of other things."

There are many ways to get wisdom. But a primary one is by praying for it. Paul prayed that the Colossians would receive wisdom. He wanted them to be full of wisdom, knowledge, and understanding. Can you imagine being so full you nearly burst? That must be *some* wisdom!

Get that, and you will succeed.

I pray for wisdom today, and wisdom tomorrow, and wisdom every day. Because you can give it. In Jesus, amen.

THEME: UNDERSTANDING

Unteachable People

People like that are proud. They don't understand any-thing. They like to argue more than they should. They can't agree about what words mean.

1 TIMOTHY 6:4

"What do you mean by 'steal'?" Andy said. "It might just be borrowing."

"You stole it," Chuck said. "It's as simple as that."

"Oh, I'll pay them someday."

"Yeah, sure." Chuck shrugged.

Andy got defensive. "Hey, you've stolen stuff!"

"Yeah," Chuck said, "but I took it back, and I don't do it anymore."

"You think you're so good. What a jerk!" With that, Andy left.

There is a kind of person who argues about every-thing. Words. Expressions. Meanings. What they did and why. And why it's okay. Even when you know it's wrong.

Avoid those people. They'll drag you down.

_____ argues with me all the time about things I know are wrong. Help me, Lord, to correct him, and to love him for you. Amen.

THEME: UNDERSTANDING

They Hear But Don't Understand

Go to your people. Say to them, "You will hear but never understand. You will see but never know what you are seeing."

ACTS 28:26

When you come to God's Word and don't believe, a strange thing happens: you hear the words, but you don't understand.

That's what happened to Paul and the Jews in the above passage. Paul quoted Isaiah, who wrote about 700 years before Christ. The people of that day were disobedient, hateful, nasty, and ugly to each other. They knew God's Word. But they didn't listen to it. Eventually something horrible happened: they ceased to understand at all. They became like animals. They just did what came natural to them.

It can happen to anyone. When we refuse to believe the truth, a curtain goes up in front of our eyes. We see the acts but don't see the truth. We hear the expressions but don't hear God's Word.

Do you come to God's Word today with a believing heart? If so, you will see as God sees.

Help me to keep believing, Father, because I know it's the only way to live. In Jesus, amen.

THEME: UNDERSTANDING

Be Sure!

Be very sure that God has appointed you to be saved. Be sure that he has chosen you. If you do everything I have just said, you will never trip and fall.

2 PETER 1:10

Every now and then it's good to take a look at your spiritual life. It's good to ask the question: Do I really belong to Jesus? Am I really a Christian?

How do you know if you're the real thing? Here are three questions to ask:

1. Do I believe in Jesus as my Lord and Savior, who died for my sins on the cross? If you say yes, you've made the right start. No one can be a Christian without believing in Jesus.
2. Have I repented of all known sin? Am I striving to live a holy life? If so, you are following him. Doing this shows the faith you have in your heart.
3. Am I trying to tell others about Jesus?

If you can say yes to these things, you are undoubtedly a Christian.

I'm a Christian, Lord. I'm sure of it. Help me to live like one. Amen.

One More Examination

Take a good look at yourselves to see if you are really believers. Test yourselves. Don't you realize that Christ Jesus is in you? Unless, of course, you fail the test!

2 CORINTHIANS 13:5

When Paul wrote to the Corinthians, he was writing to the most disobedient group of Christians of all time. Repeatedly, he told them to get their act together. He advised them to turn from sin. He warned them to lead holy lives.

He ended his second letter with the above words. He wanted the Corinthians to make sure they had the right stuff.

How do you know if you are the real thing? There's only one way: Is Jesus in you? Does he lead you to live for him?

If so, you can be sure you have the right stuff.

I need to make sure I'm a Christian, Father. Enlighten me and show me where I might be wrong. In Jesus, amen.

THEME: GOING THE DISTANCE

Keep On With It

Keep on doing those things. Give them your complete attention. Then everyone will see how you are coming along.
1 TIMOTHY 4:15

Years ago, there used to be a slogan some people used to encourage each other. They would say, "Keep on truckin'." That meant, keep on driving your spiritual truck (your body and life) and don't turn back.

If there's anything that Christians need to do it's to keep on with it. Hang in there. Stick with the program. Don't give up.

Sometimes it's hard. You wish you could just flop down, sleep, and forget you exist. That's why God gives us his rest. You don't have to struggle so much as walk. Just one step after the other.

Are you walking with him? Keep on with it.

Let me keep walking with you, Jesus—one step in front of the other. Amen.

Be Strong!

Finally, let the Lord make you strong. Depend on his mighty power.

EPHESIANS 6:10

In the first *Rocky* movie, the famous boxer has a moment when he doubts everything. He says to his girlfriend he knows he can't defeat his opponent, Apollo Creed. He says he's not even in the same class. He doesn't deserve to be in the same ring.

But he is in the same ring. And he can't give up. So he says one more thing: "I just want to go the distance."

It's a powerful scene. "Go the distance." Just last the twelve or fifteen rounds. Just keep standing. When you fall, get up. When you want to give in, refuse.

That's the Christian life. Going the distance. Being strong in Christ.

Let me go the distance for Jesus, Lord. I want to please him. Amen.

THEME: GOING THE DISTANCE

Grace

My son, be strong in the grace that is found in Christ Jesus.

2 TIMOTHY 2:1

What is grace?

It's not just something you say at the dinner table. It's an important biblical word that means "favor," "help," or "good will." The most basic definition is that it's God's favor. It's God's free gift that puts us in a right relationship with him. When God gives us grace, he removes all the barriers between us and him. He draws us close to his chest and says, "All is forgiven. You are my son. You are my daughter. I will never let you go."

Remember the parable of the prodigal son? The boy who spent his inheritance and ended up slopping pigs? He came back home, and what did his father do? He welcomed him and called for a party.

That's God. He wants us to feel welcomed, favored, loved, cared for.

That's grace. Be strong in it.

Teach me to be strong in your grace, Jesus. Help me to understand it and to apply it in my life. Amen.

THEME: GOING THE DISTANCE

God Will Keep You

God will keep you strong to the very end. Then you will be without blame on the day our Lord Jesus Christ returns.
1 CORINTHIANS 1:8

Jamal looked like he was about to cry. "What's wrong?" asked his teacher, Mrs. Gibbs.

"I'm afraid," Jamal said.

"Of what?"

"That I won't make it."

"Make what?" Mrs. Gibbs pressed.

"Make it to the end of my life as a Christian."

"Oh, you're not responsible for that," Mrs. Gibbs said. "You're just responsible for now. Today. God will get you to the end."

It's true. God doesn't expect you to figure everything out now. He'll take you step by step. And he'll get you to the end. Safely. Blamelessly.

Don't let me worry about tomorrow, Father. Let me be concerned to obey you today. Amen.

THEME: GOING THE DISTANCE

He Will Carry It Off

I am sure that the One who began a good work in you will carry it on until it is completed. That will be on the day Christ Jesus returns.

PHILIPPIANS 1:6

Did you know you're not the only one in this adventure called Christian living? Jesus is in it with you. He lives in your heart. He goes with you step by step through everything. And he intends to bring it to the right conclusion.

Many times Christians are afraid of giving up the faith. Or of sinning so bad, God kicks them out. Or of just forgetting the whole thing.

But that can never happen. God is in this with you. He's got as much to lose as you. In fact, he has more to lose. If he loses one of his children, he's broken his promise.

But he won't lose any of his children. And that includes you.

I praise you, Lord, that you promise you'll never lose me. Thanks for that assurance, because I need it. Amen.

THEME: GOING THE DISTANCE

Creation Versus Evolution

In the beginning, God created the heavens and the earth.
GENESIS 1:1

"But how do we know God created everything?" Leonard asked his friend Tibor. "The teacher says it was all evolution."

"I know," Tibor answered, "but at my church the pastor preached about it. He said that evolution fails to explain a lot of things. I mean, look at my watch. Are you going to believe it just happened? No, it was made by someone. So why should we think that monkeys and snakes and people just happened by chance?"

"But if God created everything, then he probably wants us to listen to him or something."

"Exactly," Tibor said. "That's why lots of people prefer evolution. It lets them off the hook."

"Hmm," Leonard said. "That's dangerous if there really is a God."

"You're telling me!"

Leonard was right. And so was Tibor. God did create the universe. And we have to answer to him about how we live in it.

I'm glad you're my creator, Lord. That way I don't have to worry that anything about me is made wrong. Amen.

THEME: WHO IS GOD?

The Rock

He is the Rock. His works are perfect. All of his ways are right. He is faithful. He doesn't do anything wrong. He is honest and fair.

DEUTERONOMY 32:4

Who is God? He can be summed up in one word: *rock*. He is the rock on which the whole universe rests. He is the rock that sustains the earth. He is the rock that each of us leans on.

When Moses said God is the rock, he made some other powerful statements about him.

1. His works are perfect. Nothing he does is flawed, sinful, or shabby.
2. His ways are right. He would never sin or do evil.
3. He is faithful. Loyal. He doesn't give up on anyone.
4. He doesn't do anything wrong.
5. He is honest and fair.

If he is this way, how can anyone not believe in him?

All these things about you are so great, Father. I want to stop and worship you right now by giving thanks. Thanks! Amen.

THEME: WHO IS GOD?

God's Soft Side

The LORD is tender and kind. He is gracious. He is slow to get angry. He is full of love.

PSALM 103:8

Sometimes we speak of people as having a "soft side" and a "hard side." The hard side is their "difficult-to-deal-with" nature. They're perfectionists. They're tough. They're demanding.

Then there's the soft side. No one has a softer side than God. He is tender and kind, as David says in the above psalm. Like a mom when you're sick. She's there, willing to help, taking your temperature.

He's also gracious. Willing to give. To sacrifice.

Above all, he's slow to get angry. Have you ever had a friend or relative who's always angry? God is rarely angry. But when he is, watch out.

Finally, he's full of love. He is love itself. Everything he does is done in love.

If he is this way, can anyone not love him?

If you are love, Lord, then please love others through me. That way I won't get it wrong. In Jesus, amen.

THEME: WHO IS GOD?

Always Was and Always Will Be

"I am the Alpha and the Omega, the First and the Last," says the Lord God. *"I am the One who is, and who was, and who will come. I am the Mighty One."*

REVELATION 1:8

One fellow was afraid for God. He was afraid God might get sick. Or not wake up. Or die in his sleep. Or become senile and be unable to cope. He prayed, "Take care of yourself, God. Because if anything happens to you, we're all done for."

That will never happen. God never changes. He doesn't grow old, weary, or worried. He never tires or runs out of steam.

He always was, and he always will be. You can trust that as long as God is around—and that is forever— you are safe.

Do you believe that?

Thanks for being around forever, Jesus. Sometimes I get worried about you, and now I know I don't need to. Amen.

THEME: WHO IS GOD?

God Is a Father

Our Father in heaven, may your name be honored. May your kingdom come. May what you want to happen be done on earth as it is done in heaven.

MATTHEW 6:9–10

God is the Father of all things. He began everything that exists. He created us. He made each one of us specially in our mother's womb. He crafted us and works out the circumstances of our lives to his satisfaction.

He is a Father who cares. He's no "absentee" father. He's on the scene. He's right down in our hearts. He's with us every moment of the day. He sees what we need before we need it.

He is a Father who protects. No one can touch you unless he lets them. And if he lets them, you know it's for a good reason.

If he's all these things, he's a Father who anyone would love to have as the head of the family.

I praise you, Father, for your protecting care over me. I feel good right now about it, and I plan to feel good all day about it. Amen.

THEME: WHO IS GOD?

God Is in Charge

I am the LORD. There is no other LORD. I cause light to shine. I also create darkness. I bring good times. I also create hard times. I do all of those things. I am the LORD.

ISAIAH 45:6–7

"Everything has gone wrong," Tricia said. "All my plans are done for."

"What happened, honey?" her mother asked.

"My party. No one's coming. All the kids are going to another party at the same time."

"Then let's change the time of the party!"

"Could we?"

"Of course. We're the ones who decide, don't we?"

"Now why didn't I think of that!"

When you have a problem, you can often tell your parents and find an easy solution. God's the same way. He know how to lead us to the best way of doing things.

What do you need? Go to God, ask him, and then see what happens.

Thank you that you're in charge and no one else, Jesus. I know you'll always do what's best. Amen.

THEME: WHO IS GOD?

Jesus Was God

In the beginning, the Word was already there. The Word was with God, and the Word was God. . . . The Word became a human being. He made his home with us. We have seen his glory. It is the glory of the one and only Son.

JOHN 1:1, 14

These are important verses. They link the "Word" who was God with the "Word" who became human. That's Jesus. He was the Word.

If anyone tells you Jesus was just a good man, they're wrong. If they say, he was just a prophet, they're wrong. If they say he was a crazy man who happened to know how to hoodwink people, they're wrong.

Jesus was God. The Bible says it over and over. Get that thought deep in your mind. Jesus is God. God became a man and lived among us. Jesus came to show us what God is like.

And he did a good job, don't you think?

Jesus makes you seem so much more real, Father. Thanks for sending him. Amen.

THEME: WHO IS GOD?

God Is Love

So we know that God loves us. We depend on it. God is love. Those who lead a life of love show that they are joined to God. And God is joined to them.

1 JOHN 4:16

As we come to the theme of God's love, the first thing we must realize is that God *is* love. That means everything he is and does is characterized by love. When he disciplines us, he loves us. When he saves us, he loves us. When he leads us, he leads us in love. When he lets us go through hard times, he lets us go through them in love.

In some ways that's hard to believe. How can love make a person go through hard times?

Because God sees the end from the beginning. He knows what he has to do at point A to get us to point B.

God's love is sure, perfect, and everlasting. Are you living in it now?

I know now, Lord, that everything you let happen to me is because you love me. That makes me able to hang in there despite what happens. In Jesus, amen.

THEME: GOD'S LOVE

Christ Gave All

We know what love is because Jesus Christ gave his life for us. So we should give our lives for our brothers.

1 JOHN 3:16

The main way God loved us was by sending Jesus. When Jesus faced the cross, he was afraid. But he submitted himself to God's desire. He went to the cross to save us. On it, he paid the penalty for all our sins. He lost his life because of his love for us.

Do you see the power in that? Have you ever had someone take your place when you were about to be punished? Probably not. Most of us don't want to take our own punishment, let alone someone else's. But that's what Jesus did.

And all he asks is that we believe in him. Isn't that remarkable?

Thank you for dying for me, Jesus. I could never thank you enough, but I'll try. Amen.

THEME: GOD'S LOVE

Why We Love Him

We love because he loved us first.

1 JOHN 4:19

Why does a baby love its mother? Why does a wife love her husband? Why do kids love their parents?

Often, it's because the one they love first loved them. That is, someone decided to reach out. Like the Good Samaritan, they did something nice, even when they weren't getting anything out of it.

That's what God did. He loved us long ago, before we ever existed. We existed only in his mind. But there he saw us. And there he loved us.

From the moment he put us into this world, he loved us. He put us into our families. He placed us in the country we live in. He guided the circumstances of life so that we would have a chance to believe in Jesus. And ultimately, he will take us home to be with him.

Do you love him today? Then you know why: because he first loved you.

You say you planned all my days before I even existed, Lord. So that means they must be good in your eyes, and I'll look at them that way. Amen.

THEME: GOD'S LOVE

The Awful Word

I correct and train those I love. So be sincere, and turn away from your sins.

REVELATION 3:19

"I'm sorry I have to do this, John," John's father said. "It gives me no pleasure."

"Then don't do it," John retorted.

"I'm sorry. It's for your own good."

Dad pulled out a belt and smacked John several times on the bare bottom. John began crying. "I'm sorry I did it, Dad, I'm sorry."

"I know. And maybe now you'll remember not to do it again."

No one likes discipline. It's hard. It hurts. But God loves us so much, he will not allow us to get away with sin. He'll discipline us. He'll send hard times and difficult people to bring us into line.

And he does it because he loves us too much to let us go astray.

I know I don't like it when it happens, Father, but I'm glad you discipline me. Make me a little more like Jesus today. Amen.

THEME: GOD'S LOVE

Children of God

How great is the love the Father has given us so freely! Now we can be called children of God. And that's what we really are! The world doesn't know us because it didn't know him.

1 JOHN 3:1

In 1997, Lady Diana Spencer, Princess of Wales, was killed in an auto accident. The world mourned. Many called Diana a great woman. Why? She contributed her time and fortune to many charities. She visited hurting people around the world. She touched and held babies in her lap who had AIDS. She was considered a great humanitarian. More than any of the other members of the royal family, she was loved the world over.

But royal as she was, she did not have a greater position than a Christian. What is a Christian? A child of God. A member of God's royal family. A member of the family that will reign forever and ever.

What does it mean to you to be a "child of God"? And loved by him?

Thanks for making me your child, Master. It feels great to be part of your royal family! Amen.

God's Kindness and Love

But the kindness and love of God [came when] our Savior appeared. He saved us. It wasn't because of the good things we had done. It was because of his mercy. He saved us by washing away our sins. We were born again. The Holy Spirit gave us new life.

TITUS 3:4–5

Which example shows kindness and love?

Saying, "I love you."
Stopping a firing squad from shooting a man, and then taking his place.

Obviously, the second example *shows* love. The first example is just someone saying some words.

God knows how to show us love. He doesn't just sit up there in heaven and say, "I love you" all day long. No, he came down among us in the person of Jesus and lived with us. He died for our sins. And through his Spirit, he lives in us and guides us every day.

That kind of love should get only one response. What is yours?

I know it hurt, Jesus, but thanks for taking my punishment. I'll never stop praising you for that. Amen.

THEME: GOD'S LOVE

Deep Roots

I pray that your love will have deep roots. I pray that it will have a strong foundation. May you have power with all God's people to understand Christ's love. May you know how wide and long and high and deep it is.

EPHESIANS 3:17–18

How wide is Christ's love? So wide that if it were an ocean, it would never have an end.

How long is Christ's love? Long enough to never stop loving you. So long, you can never get out ahead of it.

How high is Christ's love? Higher than the stars. So high, you can never get above and beyond it.

How deep is Christ's love? If you were to start digging today, you would dig for all eternity and never get close to the bottom, for there is no bottom to his love.

God wants you to know everything about Christ's love. As you do, you'll be amazed and grateful. Why not thank him right now for the greatness of his love?

Thank you for the greatness of your love, Lord. I feel blessed that you're with me wherever I am. In you, amen.

THEME: GOD'S LOVE

Everything About You

LORD, you have seen what is in my heart. You know all about me.

PSALM 139:1

God knows everything about you.

He knows when you hurt yourself. He knows how you skinned your knee and cried. He knows that you tried hard not to cry when you slammed your finger in the door. He knows all about it.

He knows when you grieved over the death of your dog or cat. He knows how you hurt inside.

He knows when you did a nice thing for your mom by washing the dishes when she didn't ask. He knows how you stopped two friends from quarreling.

He knows when you messed up too. The times you cursed. The times you thought hatefully. The times you were tempted.

God knows everything about you. And he still loves you. That's a powerful truth, isn't it?

I'm glad you know everything about me and still love me, Jesus. That's a pretty great brand of love. In your name, amen.

THEME: GOD KNOWS EVERYTHING

Your Thoughts Are Known, Too

You know when I sit down and when I get up. You know what I'm thinking even though you are far away.

PSALM 139:2

"I can tell what you're thinking," Sherisa said to her friend Latasha.

"You can not."

"Can too."

"What am I thinking?"

"That you wish you had jeans like me."

"Was not!"

"Was too!"

Even though we might think we know what someone is thinking, we're usually wrong. Our thoughts are private. No person can get inside of our heads.

That's good protection. If some people knew what we thought about them, they'd be angry.

But God knows your thoughts. What are your thoughts now? Do you wish God didn't know them?

Sometimes I wish you didn't know what I think, Father, but now I'm glad, because it means you know me as I really am, and still love me. Amen.

He Knows How You Live

You know when I go out to work and when I come back home. You know exactly how I live.

PSALM 139:3

"This room is a pigsty!" Clint's mother said. "I can't stand it!"

"I'm the one who lives in it," Clint said. "What's the big deal?"

"I don't want a messy house! Furthermore, it's good to keep things neat and clean."

"So what? No one will ever see it except you."

"God will, honey. And I'll tell you, God isn't pleased with this room!"

Yes, God sees how we live. Everything we do and say. Everything we think and are on the inside. We might think it would be nice if we could hide those things from God. But then no one would really understand us.

That's the beauty of God's knowledge. He knows us through to the deepest thoughts. And he understands us completely.

How do you feel about that?

No one really knows me like you, Jesus, and I'm glad. Because you also care about me infinitely. Amen.

THEME: GOD KNOWS EVERYTHING

Even Before I Speak!

LORD, even before I speak a word, you know all about it.
PSALM 139:4

Linda listened to her friend tell about the movie. As her friend talked, her mind was saying, *This is so stupid and boring. I wish I could just get out of here.*

Her friend was saying, "It was so cool. And when the ship started to sink . . ."

Linda thought, *Looks like I'll be here for the next six hours!*

Her friend said, "And then when they kissed, I was so . . ."

Linda thoughts went, *Why doesn't she just shut up?*

Do you know that God knows all about what Linda was thinking? Fortunately, her friend didn't. But think if your thoughts were broadcast on a giant screen TV behind you for everyone to see! Wouldn't you be embarrassed?

Do you know that God sees all our thoughts, and yet he still cares enough to listen to our prayers at night?

Now that's amazing!

Thank you, Lord, that you love me even though you know my wrong thoughts. In Jesus, amen.

THEME: GOD KNOWS EVERYTHING

God Knew It All from the Beginning

Before something even happens, I announce how it will end. In fact, from times long ago I announced what was still to come. I say, "My plan will succeed. I will do anything I want to do."

ISAIAH 46:10

God has told us many things that will happen at the end of time.

Earthquakes and famines will increase.

People will claim to be Jesus. There will be a great false prophet.

Christians will be persecuted. People will hate those who follow Jesus. At the same time, the world will be going along as if Jesus will never come back.

In the end, Jesus will come back and set everything right.

These things could happen in your lifetime. Be watching. God told us what will happen in the end, so that we know he really is in control of world history. And that should make us trust him all the more.

It's scary, Lord, to think about the future and all the things you have planned. But I'm glad you're the planner, and not someone else. Amen.

THEME: GOD KNOWS EVERYTHING

God Knows Your Christian Character

I know what you are doing. I know your love and your faith. I know how well you have served. I know you don't give up easily. In fact, you are doing more now than you did at first.

REVELATION 2:19

When we say God knows everything, we mean *everything*. But especially what you're doing with your life as a Christian.

In this passage, Jesus speaks to the church at a city called Pergamum. He tells them all he knows about them. But he ends the story with a problem. In the next verse, he'll tell them what dismays him about them. They had done many good things. But they had a serious black mark. Look it up to see what it is.

Sometimes you can be doing many great things for God, and still displease him. That doesn't mean he stops loving you. It just means you need to grow and change.

What do you think God knows about you right now that you need to change? Why not make that change this week?

Help me, Jesus, with my problem with _____. I know I need to change. But I need your power. Amen.

THEME: GOD KNOWS EVERYTHING

Motives, Thoughts, and Other Cool Things

You try to make yourselves look good in the eyes of other people. But God knows your hearts. What is worth a great deal among people is hated by God.

LUKE 16:15

Situation #1: A baby cries. A boy grimaces, then goes to give the baby her pacifier. The baby stops crying. The boy goes back to his TV show.

Situation #2: A baby cries. A boy shakes his head, then goes to put the pacifier back in the baby's mouth. She continues crying. He talks to her for a moment, and soon the baby quiets down. The boy goes back to his TV show.

Which boy had the right motives for what he did? The first boy heard the baby crying and thought, *I'll never get to watch my show if I don't shut her up.* The second boy heard the same baby, but thought, *Oh, I bet she lost her pacifier. I'll get it for her.*

God knows your motives for doing things. That's why we have to test our motives and make sure they're pure. What motives do you notice in your heart when you do something? Even something good?

I'm glad you know my motives, Father. That means you know my heart even when I fail. In Jesus' name, amen.

THEME: GOD KNOWS EVERYTHING

Held in His Power

You are all around me. You are behind me and in front of me. You hold me in your power.

PSALM 139:5

Have you ever seen the commercial that says, "You're in good hands with Allstate?" It pictures a huge pair of hands. In the hands is a little family, their house, and all their possessions.

That might be a good commercial for God. We're in his hands. We are held in his power.

Do you realize what that means? God—right now—is holding you. No one can do a thing to you unless he lets them. He holds others too. In fact, everyone is in the power and hands of God.

That's great comfort to anyone who feels alone. Do you ever feel alone? Look up. God is holding you.

Sometimes I feel alone, Lord, but I know you're holding me. And that makes me want to talk with you. In Jesus, amen.

THEME: GOD IS EVERYWHERE

You Can't Get Away

How can I get away from your Spirit? Where can I go to escape from you? If I go up to the heavens, you are there. If I lie down in the deepest parts of the earth, you are also there.

PSALM 139:7–8

"I'll run and hide and you'll never find me!"

Ever say those words to your mom or dad when you were angry? It's not hard to find such a place. Moms and dads don't know everything. Kids can hide in spots that they'll never find.

But we can't hide from God. Have you committed a sin? God knows about it. He saw all of it. You can't run, and you can't hide. The only thing you can do is turn to him, repent, and ask his forgiveness.

What has God seen you do?

Lord, I know you see everything I do. Please forgive me when I do wrong. Amen.

THEME: GOD IS EVERYWHERE

Held Close

Suppose I were to rise with the sun in the east and then cross over to the west where it sinks into the ocean. Your hand would always be there to guide me. Your right hand would still be holding me close.

PSALM 139:9–10

Have you ever felt sick and lonely and then your mom came and hugged you close? Wasn't that a warm spot? Wouldn't that be a nice place to stay?

Moms have lots of warm spots. They hold us and we feel good.

God is like a mom sometimes. The way he holds us, though, is through moms and dads and others. When they hold us close, we should realize that God is also holding us close like that. You may not feel him or see him or even hear him. But he's there.

We call this truth God's "omnipresence." It means he's "everywhere present."

God is here. Now. In this room. By your bed or desk. Listening. Waiting for you to come to him and speak.

I'm so glad you're here, Father. What would you like to talk about? In Jesus, amen.

THEME: GOD IS EVERYWHERE

God Knows the Dark, Too

Suppose I were to say, "I'm sure the darkness will hide me. The light around me will become as dark as night." Even that darkness would not be dark to you. The night would shine like the day, because darkness is like light to you.

PSALM 139:11–12

A little boy called out at night, "Daddy, hurry, I'm scared."

When his dad arrived, he told the boy not to be afraid.

"But the dark is so dark," the boy said.

"But God is here. God is here in the dark. He knows all about you."

"Yes," said the boy, "I know. But I need someone with skin on."

That's an old story, but how true. We all need someone "with skin on" sometimes.

Have you ever felt afraid in the dark? God is there in the dark, too. He knows how you feel. Call to him and he'll speak. If you'll listen.

I don't like the dark, Master, but now that I know you're there, it makes me feel better. Amen.

THEME: GOD IS EVERYWHERE

You Will Find Him

They would find him even though he is not far from any of us. In him we live and move and exist. As some of your own poets have also said, "We are his children."

ACTS 17:27–28

"I just don't know where God is," Kenley said to her youth pastor. "I wish I could see him."

"You can," the youth pastor said. "But you must see him with spiritual eyes."

"How do I get spiritual eyes?"

"By faith. By reaching out to him with your heart."

"How do I do that?"

"Just call on him. He'll answer, if you're sincere."

Yes, anyone can contact God. All you need to do to find him is to seek him with your heart. He promises to answer anyone and everyone who does that.

Teach me to seek you with all my heart, Lord. I know you seek me with all yours. In Jesus' name, amen.

THEME: GOD IS EVERYWHERE

It Must Come from the Heart

When you look for me with all your heart, you will find me.

JEREMIAH 29:13

What does it mean to seek God with "all your heart"?

The heart is the center of your spiritual being. It's the place where you think and feel and have motives and desires. It's the deepest part of your being. And it's the part God most wants us to share with him.

Why? Because our hearts are who we really are. When we give from the heart, we're giving from the deepest, most sincere, and most godly part of ourselves. The heart can't hide anything. It always tells the truth.

God wants our hearts because that's the part of us that is most like him. That's the part that talks to him and learns from him. That's the part that worships and loves him.

Are you seeking him with all your heart? If not, why not? And if so, have you found him?

Open my heart to your Word, Jesus, that I might walk in your light. Amen.

THEME: GOD IS EVERYWHERE

No One Is Far from God

The LORD blocks the sinful plans of the nations. He keeps them from doing what they want to do. But the plans of the LORD stand firm forever. What he wants to do will last for all time.

PSALM 33:10–11

Have you ever wondered what God thinks of Saddam Hussein, the evil president of Iraq? Or of the leaders of China, who persecute Christians? Or of other people in the world who have great power and use it to hurt others?

Don't worry about them. They're in God's hands. No leader can do anything unless God lets him. He may think he's getting away with murder. He may think he's in charge. But he's not. It's when such people really believe they have power like God that they're in the greatest danger. God sometimes has to humble them to help them to see.

God cares about Saddam Hussein. And China's leaders. And everyone else. If they seek him, he's not so far away that he will not come and show them his love. All they have to do is ask.

It's amazing that you care so much about everyone, Father. Help me to tell the world that message. Amen.

THEME: GOD IS EVERYWHERE

The Trinity

May the grace shown by the Lord Jesus Christ, and the love that God has given us, and the sharing of life brought about by the Holy Spirit be with you all.

2 Corinthians 13:14

Scripture contains many mysteries. These are truths that we believe but may not understand. One of the first of such truths is the Trinity. God is three persons: the Father, the Son, and the Spirit. But he is not three Gods. He is one God who exists as three Persons.

Does that make sense? To many people it doesn't. But there are many things in nature that exist in threes: water, which can be liquid, solid, or gas. An egg, which has a yolk, white, and shell.

Still, that doesn't explain the Trinity. But we don't have to explain it. We accept it. After all, if we could completely explain God, we'd be greater than God. And where would that leave us?

I'm glad I don't have to understand everything about you, Lord, to believe in you. I'm also glad that you're going to teach me more every day. Amen.

Inspiration of Scripture

God has breathed life into all of Scripture.

2 TIMOTHY 3:16

A second mystery in Scripture is the idea that the Bible is God's Word. But it was written by men. How can the writings and thoughts of men be God's perfect Word?

We try to explain it by saying that the Holy Spirit worked through the men to write what he wanted to say. But that's not the whole story. Why? Because those men had personalities. They had likes and dislikes. They had their own ideas. How did God make sure that what they said was truly his Word?

Again, we can't completely understand. As some say, "God works in mysterious ways." The wonder of it is that God has given us his Word. And he did it by using people to write it.

That means he can use you to accomplish great things too. Are you encouraged?

Do some great thing through me one day, Father. And whatever it is, I'll thank you for it. In Jesus, amen.

THEME: THE MYSTERIES OF GOD

Jesus: God and Man

In his very nature he was God. But he did not think that being equal with God was something he should hold on to. Instead, he made himself nothing. He took on the very nature of a servant. He was made in human form.

PHILIPPIANS 2:6–7

A third tremendous mystery in the Bible is Jesus. In this passage, he was "in very nature" God. That means he was God through and through. But he decided to do something. He made himself a servant and became a human being.

Was he still God? Yes. Was he a real person with real thoughts and feelings and a body? Yes.

How can this be? It's something of a mystery. But if God were to become a man, don't you think Jesus is the perfect description of what that man would be like?

It is, and we will worship him forever for it.

If Jesus was like me, then I know he understands me. That's greatly encouraging. Thank you, Lord. Amen.

THEME: THE MYSTERIES OF GOD

God Is in Charge, But We Make Real Choices

He showed us the mystery of his plan. It was in keeping with what he wanted to do. It was what he had planned through Christ.

EPHESIANS 1:9

Here's another mystery. We often say that God is in control. He's in charge of the world and the universe. Nothing catches him off guard. He has planned everything that will ever happen.

On the other hand, people make choices. Does God force them into his plans? No. Does God demand that they listen to him? No.

Then how can God be in charge? These people are doing what they want.

That's the mystery: we do what we want. At the same time, God had it all planned from the beginning of time.

What does that mean for you? It means God can really answer your prayers. He can help you anywhere, anytime. He really is in charge. And you really have the responsibility to make right choices.

Lord, let me make right choices. Fill me with your Spirit so I'll know what most pleases you in my life today. Amen.

THEME: THE MYSTERIES OF GOD

God in us

God has chosen to make known to them the glorious riches of that mystery. He has made it known among those who aren't Jews. And here is what it is. Christ is in you. He is your hope of glory.

COLOSSIANS 1:27

This is one of the most incredible mysteries of all. We are people. We have souls and spirits. We are unique, with personalities and choices and desires.

At the same time, God the Holy Spirit lives in our hearts. He is inside of our most personal selves. He leads us. He speaks to us. He opens us up to serving him.

How can we be ourselves, and yet God is in us?

Again, it's a mystery. But it means that none of us is ever alone. You have a person inside of you who understands you completely. You have a person who will be with you always. What is your response to that?

Thanks for living inside me, Jesus. I hope I'll please you today as you look out through my eyes. Amen.

A Big God Cares for a Small Sparrow

The One who came down is the same as the One who went up higher than all the heavens. He did it in order to fill all of creation.

EPHESIANS 4:10

In this passage, it says that Jesus "fills all of creation." In Matthew 10:29, Jesus says not a single sparrow falls to the ground "without the Father knowing about it." How can God be that big and care about something that small at the same time?

God is spirit. Unlike any other being in all of creation, he has powers and abilities we can't comprehend. His Spirit fills all of the universe and everything else. He is without end. At the same time, his Spirit touches everything in his creation. Just as he is bigger than it, he is also able to be in contact with all of it.

What does that mean for you? Just this: when you pray, God gives you his complete attention. When you have a need, he's there, ready to help. God's bigness makes him able to help everyone everywhere. And his attention to the smallest detail enables him to be personal to *you*.

I'm pretty little, Father, and I give thanks that you're little enough to work in me. Amen.

THEME: THE MYSTERIES OF GOD

Sinful, Yet Perfect

We preach about him. With all the wisdom we have, we warn and teach everyone. When we bring them to God, we want them to be perfect as people who belong to Christ.

COLOSSIANS 1:28

A final mystery concerns our sinfulness. We know that we do things wrong. We know we make mistakes. We know that at times we even sin willfully. That is, we know it's wrong, but we do it anyway.

Everyone has these kinds of problems.

At the same time, God assures us that he will make us perfect. How will he do that if he starts with sinful people? How will he stop us from ever sinning again?

Again, Scripture doesn't explain this. It just says it's so. But doesn't it encourage you? One day you will be perfect. And your goodness will last forever.

I'm looking forward to the day when I'm perfect, Jesus. Until then, keep forgiving me and making me like yourself. Amen.

You Can Depend on It

Finally, let the Lord make you strong. Depend on his mighty power.

EPHESIANS 6:10

God is powerful. In fact, the term we use in theology is "omnipotent." That means "possessing all power" or "every power." We call him "All-powerful."

Can God really do anything? Yes, anything that conforms to his character and purpose and glory. He can't sin. He won't do stupid things (like make a rock so big even he couldn't lift it!). He isn't in the business of performing. (So don't expect him to cut a best-selling song, or come down and win the Super Bowl.)

Thus, while God is all-powerful and can do anything he chooses to do, what he chooses to do is not necessarily what you might wish. But one thing is sure: he can make you strong, as this Scripture says. He can help you in times of trouble. Depend on him, and you'll never find him weak.

Help me to learn to depend on you, Lord, for everything. In Jesus, amen.

THEME: GOD'S POWER

All You Need

God's power has given us everything we need to lead a godly life.

2 PETER 1:3

What does it take to live right?

It takes desire. It takes commitment. And it takes God's power and help.

You can't do it alone.

A boy stood out in the backyard with his dad. Suddenly, his dad said, "Jamie, lift up that rock there and bring it over here."

Jamie obeyed, but the rock was too big. He couldn't lift it. His father said, "Are you using all your resources?"

Jamie looked around, then at his arms. "Yeah."

"No, you're not," his dad said. "You haven't used me."

With Dad helping, Jamie was able to lift the rock. It's the same thing with us. Sometimes we forget to get God involved. We only pray after things are messed up. Instead, try making God part of everything you do. Guaranteed, life will be simpler and easier.

I invite you into everything I do today, Father. Wherever we go, I want you to lead. Amen.

THEME: GOD'S POWER

Jesus in White

We told you about the time our Lord Jesus Christ came with power. But we didn't make up stories when we told you about it. With our own eyes we saw him in all his majesty.
2 PETER 1:16

Peter is talking here about the time he, James, and John went with Jesus up a mountain. There, Jesus appeared with Moses and Elijah. His garments became radiant white, brighter than the sun. Presumably, his face and form changed too. They became beautiful, perfect, angelic, divine.

One day God intends to do the same thing to you. If someone saw you after you rose from the dead, he would worship you as God himself. You will be that powerful and look that perfect.

Can't you wait for that day to come?

I don't want anyone to worship me, Jesus, but I look forward to being perfect and powerful. Make that day come soon. Amen.

THEME: GOD'S POWER

The Indestructible Life

He has not become a priest because of a rule about his family line. He has become a priest because of his powerful life.
HEBREWS 7:16

In one version of the Bible, this verse says Jesus became an eternal priest because of "the power of an indestructible life." What does that mean?

Jesus will always be our priest. That is, he represents us to God. He goes before God the Father and acts as a go-between. Anything we need and want, Jesus requests. God grants it to him because he is God's Son. We don't come to God on our own merits. That is, we don't pretend that we deserve anything from him. But because we believe in Jesus, he has become our friend and middleman.

Because he has an indestructible life, we never need fear that God will ever punish us for our sins. When you believe in Jesus, your sins are gone. Forgiven. Washed away. Cleansed. Forever.

I praise you, Lord, that my sins are forgiven. I pray for _____, that you would open his eyes so that he could see the same truth. Amen.

THEME: GOD'S POWER

The Good News Is Powerful

Our good news didn't come to you only in words. It came with power. It came with the Holy Spirit's help.

1 THESSALONIANS 1:5

"I don't think Gary will believe this, Dad," Philip said. "He just doesn't believe religious stuff."

"All you can do is try, son," Philip's dad said. "You never know what can happen."

"But I'm not good at arguing. And I don't know all the Bible verses."

"Just tell him about Jesus. And then let Jesus work in him. That's all God expects."

Have you ever been frustrated about how unbelievers don't accept your faith as real? Or your belief in Jesus as important?

Think again. You don't have to convince anyone. The gospel is powerful. The Spirit of God works in people's hearts. All God wants us to do is go and tell it to them.

Can you do that?

Teach me to witness to others, Father, and not to be afraid. I know you're with me. Just make me feel your presence. Amen.

THEME: GOD'S POWER

God's Two Witnesses

These witnesses have power to close up the sky. Then it will not rain while they are prophesying. They also have power to turn the waters into blood. And they can strike the earth with every kind of plague as often as they want to.

REVELATION 11:6

In the book of Revelation, the apostle John talks about two witnesses. These will be two prophets who preach to the world during the end times. Many people will be converted through their message. But many others will turn against them.

What you should notice is the power of these two men. They can shut off the rain. They can turn water into blood. They can strike the earth with plagues.

Who is the power behind the two witnesses? God. Showing his power is his way of trying to convince people he's real.

Have you seen God's power today, in any way? How?

Let me see a little piece of your power today, Jesus. Work in me! Amen.

The Roar in Heaven

After these things I heard a roar in heaven. It sounded like a huge crowd shouting. "Hallelujah! Salvation and glory and power belong to our God."

REVELATION 19:1

Another passage in Revelation talks about God's personal works in the world. It reduces them to three:

Salvation—what Jesus did on the cross to make eternal life possible.

Glory—how God shows himself off to the world, through his Word, through Jesus, through believers, and finally through himself.

Power—the fact that God works among us.

The Bible shows God as a God of power. He created the world with just a few words from his lips. He parted the Red Sea. He sent Jesus to heal, raise the dead, and speak words that have lasted thousands of years. He also works in the lives of his people today.

Have you seen God work in your life lately? Why not spend some time in prayer and ask him to show you what he's doing?

I want you to work in my life today, Master. Just don't go knocking down all my walls at once! Amen.

THEME: GOD'S POWER

Secret Wisdom

No, we speak about God's secret wisdom. His wisdom has been hidden. But before time began, God planned that his wisdom would bring us heavenly glory.

1 CORINTHIANS 2:7

"I don't get it," Annie said. "Why should Jesus have to die for me? It doesn't make sense."

"But he had to die for our sins. He died in our place," Kate answered.

"He shouldn't have had to *die*," Annie argued.

"I wish I could make you understand," Kate sighed.

Kate's problem is a common one. When we explain the gospel to people, they don't always understand. Parts of it seem foolish. Why is this? Because God's wisdom is hidden from unbelieving hearts. If you don't believe, you won't see the truth. You have to believe to see.

That's why God's wisdom sometimes is very different from our common sense. But that doesn't mean it's wrong. God has chosen to reveal his wisdom to some people and hide it from others. Has God shown you the truth?

I want to tell _____ about you this week, Lord. Open the doors and show me the way. In Jesus' name, amen.

THEME: GOD'S WISDOM

God's Plans

"I know the plans I have for you," announces the LORD. "I want you to enjoy success. I do not plan to harm you. I will give you hope for the years to come."

JEREMIAH 29:11

God has plans for you. Did you know that?

Yes, he does. He's got it all figured out. He's laid out your life from beginning to end. Then he put into it all the good things he saw would help you grow. That's why God continually tells us to trust him when things appear to go wrong. It's all just part of his plan to make us like Jesus.

That's the point, isn't it? God's plan isn't designed to make us happy, or healthy, or wealthy, or successful. God's plan is to make us like Jesus.

So what is he doing in your life today?

I know all those things like wealth and health are not always your plan, Jesus. Help me to accept what is your plan for me without complaining. Amen.

THEME: GOD'S WISDOM

Everything Works for Good

We know that in all things God works for the good of those who love him. He appointed them to be saved in keeping with his purpose.

ROMANS 8:28

"I don't see how this can be for good," Gillian said. "My mom is sick. She might die. How can that be good?"

Shona responded, "You might not see it now. But someday you will. We just have to trust God's Word."

"That's what they always say," Gillian said. "He'll have to prove it to me to convince me."

Gillian is a typical case. A lot of Christians don't see the "good" in God's plan. But he really does work things for good, if we love him. We might not see the good today or tomorrow, or even for several years. But God usually shows it to us eventually.

We just have to trust him. Do you trust him? Are you trusting him today?

Let me see the good in the situation with _____, Lord. I want to trust you no matter what happens. Amen.

The Way God Deals With People

How very rich are God's wisdom and knowledge! How he judges is more than we can understand! The way he deals with people is more than we can know!

ROMANS 11:33

Adolph Hitler was the ruler of Germany from about 1934 to 1945. He fixed Germany's economic problems, and everyone in Germany loved him. But then he began to do horrible things. He used his armies to attack other countries. And he tried to kill off all the Jews. He was a wicked, wicked man.

Ultimately, the United States, Great Britain, and Russia stopped Hitler. He committed suicide in his Berlin bunker just before the Russians reached him.

Why did God let a man like Hitler exist? There could be many reasons. But one of them was to show his wisdom. God took a powerful man and country and stopped them in their tracks. He's done it all through history. When people defy him, they get into trouble.

God uses his wisdom in dealing with all people. He will use it in dealing with you. Are you making it easy or hard on him?

Lord, help me to see your wisdom at work in the world. Amen.

THEME: GOD'S WISDOM

Just Ask

If any of you need wisdom, ask God for it. He will give it to you. God gives freely to everyone. He doesn't find fault.
JAMES 1:5

"I don't know what to do," Adam said. "Nothing works. I'll never get out of this problem."

Bryce sympathized. But he suggested, "Why don't we ask God for wisdom about this? Maybe he'll tell you something you haven't thought of."

Adam was interested. They both stopped what they were doing and prayed. Afterwards, Adam said, "I wonder what he'll tell me. Or what he'll do."

"Wait and see," Bryce said. "We can only be sure of one thing: he will do something!"

That's the truth. When you ask God for wisdom, he gives it. It may not be wisdom you want to hear, but he'll supply it. Just ask.

I trust you, Father, to give me wisdom for things happening in school right now. Help me to do what's right even if it hurts. In Jesus' name, amen.

THEME: GOD'S WISDOM

The Wisdom God Gives

But the wisdom that comes from heaven is pure. That's the most important thing about it. And that's not all. It also loves peace. It thinks about others. It obeys. It is full of mercy and good fruit. It is fair. It doesn't pretend to be what it is not.

JAMES 3:17

What kind of wisdom does God give us? Look at the list above:

It's pure. It's not tainted or laced with poison.

It's peace-loving. It promotes good relationships.

It thinks about others. It's not self-centered or out for itself.

It obeys. It does the truth, no matter what.

It's full of mercy and good fruit. That is, it gives us just what we need.

It's fair. It never takes sides.

It's sincere. It doesn't fake it.

That's good stuff. Are you seeking it?

Fill me with your wisdom, Jesus. I want to burst with it today! Amen.

THEME: GOD'S WISDOM

Wisdom from Heaven

I pray to the God of our Lord Jesus Christ. God is the glorious Father. I keep asking him to give you the wisdom and understanding that come from the Holy Spirit. I want you to know God better.

EPHESIANS 1:17

Wisdom is the power to solve problems. All kinds of problems. Personal problems. Family problems. School problems. Church problems. If you have a problem, God has the wisdom to solve it.

Sometimes God gives us his wisdom in bits and pieces. We have to do something before we get the next installment. But as we obey, he supplies.

Sometimes God gives his wisdom only after much prayer. He lets us try several different things on our own. But when we pray, he answers.

Sometimes God gives his wisdom only after we've thought and prayed and worked some things through. That takes time.

If you need wisdom, God has it for you. Seek him and he'll give you what you need.

I have a tough problem to solve, Lord. Please give me your wisdom to deal with it. In Jesus, amen.

THEME: GOD'S WISDOM

Perfect Peace and Hope

May the God who gives hope fill you with great joy. May you have perfect peace as you trust in him. May the power of the Holy Spirit fill you with hope.

ROMANS 15:13

Trusting God is a little like jumping into your father's arms in the dark. A little boy got scared one night on his top bunk. It was dead dark outside. No stars. No moon. Pitch black. And then his light went out.

He started yelling that he was scared, and his father rushed into the room. "Jump into my arms," the dad said. "I'm right here."

"But I can't see you."

"I can see you. Just jump and you'll be okay."

The boy hesitated, then he leaped. His dad caught him. "See, that wasn't so bad, was it?"

"I guess," the boy said.

God wants us to trust him even though we can't see him. He assures us, "I am with you. I'm right here. Just hang tough."

I wouldn't jump that easily, I know, Lord, if I was in that situation. But I hope you'll help me to trust you wherever I am. Amen.

THEME: TRUSTING GOD

A Trusting Person

May the LORD reward you for what you have done. May the God of Israel bless you richly. You have come to him to find safety under his care.

RUTH 2:12

Ruth was a great Old Testament saint. She could have left her mother-in-law, Naomi, but she didn't. Ruth had lost her husband, Naomi's son. And Naomi had lost her other son and her husband while they traveled in the land of Moab. After losing her whole family, Naomi decided to go back to Israel. Ruth wanted to come with her. Naomi tried to stop her, but Ruth told her, "Your God will be my God. Your people will be my people."

Because of her trust in God, Naomi spoke the words above. Ruth had found safety in God and in doing his will.

Christians find safety in this world only in God. Don't trust in guns, or money, or your house. God alone is worthy of complete trust.

Keep me from trusting the world, Jesus. Let me learn to trust you and be wary of the world's ways. Amen.

THEME: TRUSTING GOD

Money and Trust

Command people who are rich in this world not to be proud. Tell them not to put their hope in riches. Wealth is so uncertain. Command those who are rich to put their hope in God. He richly provides us with everything to enjoy.

1 TIMOTHY 6:17

Harry held up the money. "I got it for my birthday," he said. "A hundred dollars."

Ted had never seen a hundred-dollar bill before. It looked like it could buy anything. As they went to the store, they talked about all the things Harry might buy. But when they got to the store, they found out that the Sony Playstation Harry wanted was more than a hundred dollars.

"I can't get it," Harry wailed.

"Sometimes money isn't enough," Ted answered.

Money will never be enough. Some people who are rich in this world think nothing can touch them. But they're wrong. Only God is the true source of hope and safety.

Are you trusting in him, or in something else?

Father, help me to trust in you only, not in money. Thank you for giving me everything I need. Amen.

THEME: TRUSTING GOD

My Rock and Fort

My LORD is my rock and my fort.... I go to him for safety. He is like a shield to me. He's the power that saves me. He's my place of safety. I go to him for help. He's my Savior.
2 SAMUEL 22:2–3

King David was a guy who knew how to trust God. But he learned it through hard experiences. When he spoke these words above, he was old. He had learned a lot in his life. But in his early days, he had some times when he failed to trust God.

- When King Saul pursued him and tried to kill him.
- When he played a madman in the Philistines' court.
- When he committed sin with Bathsheba and had her husband killed.

We learn trust through finding out what happens when we don't trust. God lets us fail sometimes when we're young so that later in life we won't fail. In what ways can you trust God today?

I pray that the missionaries from our church, the _____, will trust you today and always, Lord. Refresh and keep them strong. Amen.

THEME: TRUSTING GOD

God's Faithful Love

But I trust in your faithful love. My heart is filled with joy because you will save me.

PSALM 13:5

Katrina took the Nintendo cassette in her hand. *I could steal it so easily*, she thought. All she had to do was put it in her pocket. Her friend Sara would never suspect her.

As she clutched the cassette, though, she remembered the verse she'd learned in church the previous Sunday. What if she trusted God about this? What if she waited for God to do something? Maybe she'd get the game as a present. Or maybe she'd find another game. What should she do?

Sara came in. "Mom just told me," she said. "Everyday after school you can come over while your mom's at work. We can play the games together."

Katrina was amazed. Now she could play the game as much as she wanted. Was that God's answer?

She thanked the Lord for not letting her make a dreadful mistake. And for providing a better way.

Show me the right way, Father, even when I don't want to do it. Amen.

THEME: TRUSTING GOD

God Never Deserts Us

LORD, those who know you will trust in you. You have never deserted those who look to you.

PSALM 9:10

Cal lay on the ground moaning. "I think it's broken, Max. Broken!"

Max touched the leg. "I'll have to go for help."

"That'll take hours. Don't leave me, please."

Cal looked around at the trees of the forest. They were camping in the woods, miles from home. Cal had climbed a tree and fallen. Now it looked like his leg was broken.

"Let's pray," Max said. "You know God will never desert us, right? And neither will I."

After praying both boys felt better. Minutes later, they heard a noise and looked up. It was a man!

"We're saved!" Max cried.

Trust is a matter of telling God you know he's there. God promises to be with us through everything in life. If we trust him, we can know that he will help.

Something happened recently that I don't understand, Lord. Please help me through it. In Jesus' name, amen.

THEME: TRUSTING GOD

November

25

Don't Be Troubled

Do not let your hearts be troubled. Trust in God. Trust in me also.

JOHN 14:1

The last night before Jesus' crucifixion, he talked with his disciples. He told them he would die. He told them he would rise again. But none of them understood. Then he gave them the above words.

"Don't be troubled. Trust in God."

It's so easy to be troubled in this world. So many things can go wrong. You can lose all your money. Your parents can lose their jobs. A relative might die. A criminal might attack your family. Your car could break down in a strange place.

But Jesus assures us: "Trust in God."

Why? Because God loves us. He cares. And he has the power to help us no matter where we are, no matter how bad the situation is.

Are you trusting God for everything? Why not turn it all over to him today and then wait to see what he does tomorrow?

I pray for _____. He's sick, Lord, and he needs your healing hand. Help him trust you in this time. In Jesus, amen.

THEME: TRUSTING GOD

God Is Holy

LORD, who among the gods is like you? Who is like you? You are majestic and holy. Your glory fills me with wonder. You do wonderful miracles.

EXODUS 15:11

Holiness is one of the most difficult of all Bible truths to teach. What does it mean? How is it practical to us?

Holiness means that God is utterly separate from us. He is utterly different. That difference is sinlessness, perfection, purity. He never lets himself be used or employed in anything that is wrong or evil. He cannot commit evil. He cannot even think evil. And he cannot look on anything that is evil.

Then how can he look at us? If God was only holy, he couldn't. But God made a way for him to deal with us. Jesus. When Jesus died on the cross, he made it possible for the holy God to be our friend, our leader, our comforter.

God's holiness means he would never do wrong. And he wants us to become that way, too.

I'm glad you're holy, Father, and could never do wrong. That gives me great confidence. In Jesus' name, amen.

THEME: HOLINESS

Lead Lives of Holiness

Pray for kings. Pray for all who are in authority. Pray that we will live peaceful and quiet lives. And pray that we will be godly and holy.

1 TIMOTHY 2:2

Do you ever struggle for things to pray for? Sometimes teachers ask, "What does anyone need to pray about?" And the class is silent. No one has a thing. Except Lori, who wants to pray for her sick puppy!

Perhaps, and that's not wrong. But there are many things to pray for. This verse gives us several:

Pray for your leaders and those in authority. That they will rule rightly. That they will be honest.

Pray that we can live peaceful and quiet lives. No noise for us.

Pray that we will be godly and holy. Oooh, that's a tough one. But that's what God wants us to ask for.

Are you ready for him to begin making you holy?

I don't know how to be holy, Jesus, but if that's the way you are, that's the way I want to be. In your name, amen.

THEME: HOLINESS

Do Your Part

Our parents trained us for a little while. They did what they thought was best. But God trains us for our good. He wants us to share in his holiness.

HEBREWS 12:10

"Everything went wrong," Joel said. "She asked every question I didn't know the answer to. I flunked."

"Did you study?" his mom asked.

"Well, yeah. Sort of."

"If you didn't study, what did you expect?"

"But Mom, I prayed that God would help me. That's what they say in Sunday school. And he didn't."

"You mean you want God to help you get an A, but you don't want to study?"

"Well, yeah!"

"That's not the way God works. Study, and then he will help you. That's the way he works."

Do you want to grow in holiness? Then do your part, and God will do his.

Let me always do my part, Father, so you can do yours. Amen.

THEME: HOLINESS

Seeing the Lord

Try your best to live in peace with everyone. Try to be holy. Without holiness no one will see the Lord.

HEBREWS 12:14

Have you ever thought what an incredible thing it would be to see God's face? Do you know the Bible says we will see his face?

Yes, in Revelation 22:4. "They will see his [God's] face"!

But only certain people will be allowed. Who? Those who are holy. Those who have entrusted themselves to Jesus.

You see, an amazing thing happened when you accepted Jesus. First, God forgave you for everything. No more sins. Next, God gave you eternal life. You will live forever. Finally, God put Jesus' perfection and righteousness on you. When God sees you, he sees all the greatness and majesty of Jesus, for you are "in" him.

In Jesus, we become holy in two ways: by believing in him, and by following him. Are you doing those things?

I'm so glad I will see your face someday, Lord. Make me holy for that great day. Amen.

THEME: HOLINESS

Heart Pollution

Dear friends, we have these promises from God. So let us make ourselves pure from everything that pollutes our bodies and spirits. Let us be completely holy. We want to honor God.

2 CORINTHIANS 7:1

You've heard of air pollution. And environmental pollution. Ocean pollution. Water pollution.

What about heart pollution? Do you know what that is?

It's hatred. It's lying. It's prejudice and bigotry. It's wanting what others possess. It's complaining. It's grumbling and arguing and fighting with anyone and everyone.

Those things pollute the heart. They make it unfit for God to look into.

Do you know how you get a clean heart? First, by believing in Jesus. He cleanses us through and through. Second, by confessing all known sin. Third, by trying to live right in God's eyes. By controlling our thoughts.

When you do those things, God is pleased.

Don't let me pollute my heart, Jesus. Help me to have a heart that you like to live in. Amen.

THEME: HOLINESS

Be Holy, As God Is Holy

The one who chose you is holy. So you should be holy in all that you do. It is written, "Be holy, because I am holy."
1 PETER 1:15–16

Why does God want us to be holy? Because that's what he has always intended. That's the way he made us.

Did you know that when God first made us, we were holy? Adam and Eve were sinless. They were like God. But when they sinned, they fell from that high position. They lost their goodness and perfection. They became sinners.

Ever since then, every person ever born is a sinner. He can only stop being a sinner and become a saint by trusting Christ and following him.

God wants us to be like him. Why? So he can point to us whenever anyone asks and say, "That is what I'm like."

God wants us to be little images of him so that his universe is populated with people who love, give, sacrifice, care, and live in peace.

Make me holy, Lord, and help me to want to be holy, too. In Jesus, amen.

THEME: HOLINESS

God Will Use You

Suppose people stay away from what is not honorable. Then the Master will be able to use them for honorable purposes. They will be made holy. They will be ready to do any good work.

2 TIMOTHY 2:21

"I don't think God could ever use me," Jason said.

"Why?" asked Roger.

"I'm too messed up."

"You know what to do then, don't you?" Roger asked.

"No, what?"

"Get unmessed up!"

Right! Do you ever wish God would use you in great works like he did Peter, Paul, Matthew, and Mark? God is not going to rewrite Scripture through you. But he can do other things. Lead your friends to Jesus. Visit shut-ins at the nursing home. Help with a service project, painting or cleaning. Be a great student in your school. Offer your friends a listening ear. God will use you, if you let him. If you let him make you holy!

I want you to use me in building your kingdom, Father. Don't let me lose sight of what it means to live for you. Amen.

THEME: HOLINESS

Not Even the Heavens Can Hold Him

But will you really live on earth? After all, the heavens can't hold you. In fact, even the highest heavens can't hold you. So this temple I've built certainly can't hold you.

1 KINGS 8:27

Ever wonder how big God is? Big as a mountain? Big as the sun? Big as our galaxy, the Milky Way? Big as the universe?

It's hard to imagine. This verse, though, tells us how great and big God is. The heavens can't contain him. That is, he's bigger than space, bigger than the universe, bigger than everything else in existence. He is infinite.

Can you imagine that? What's the biggest thing you know of? The universe, undoubtedly. We haven't even seen how far out it goes. And yet, God fills all of it.

If God is that big, then what's he doing being concerned about me? That's the mystery! And the truth is that he is so concerned, he sent his Son to die for us. He's big, but not so big that he doesn't have time to care for us!

It makes me happy that you're so great, Jesus, because you're my God and I'm part of your family. In you, amen.

THEME: THE GREATNESS OF GOD

More Wonderful Than the Angels

God is highly respected among his holy angels. He's more wonderful than all those who are around him.

PSALM 89:7

What might happen if an angel appeared to you? Would you be scared? Would you be curious? Would you shake hands?

Most of us aren't sure what we would do if an angel appeared to us. But Scripture teaches that angels are majestic creations of God. They're beautiful, perfect, powerful, amazing to look at.

Yet an angel is nothing compared to God. What must it be like to look on God's face? To hear his voice? To have him walk with you down the road?

God has a way of letting you know what this might be like. Think of Jesus. He's God in human form. When you think of what God is like, just think of Jesus. And you'll have a clear picture.

Jesus, you're the perfect picture of God to me. Help me to keep you in my mind and heart. Amen.

THEME: THE GREATNESS OF GOD

No One Can Understand

Lord, you are great. You are really worthy of praise. No one can completely understand how great you are.

Psalm 145:3

A young man stood in a church listening to a great preacher. When question and answer time came, he asked, "How could the Jews wander in the wilderness and not get hungry, their clothes not wear out, their sandals not wear out?"

The preacher thought a moment, and then said, "God!"

The young man answered, "Now I understand, sir."

The preacher replied, "No, son, no one understands. No one."

When you read the Bible, you'll read some amazing things. But the answer to how they could be always is "God!" How could God do them? We don't know. We only know that he did, and that it is marvelous in our eyes!

I'm glad you did great things in the Bible, Father. It gives me something to look up to and hope you'll do them again! Amen.

THEME: THE GREATNESS OF GOD

No Limit to God's Understanding

Great is our Lord. His power is mighty. There is no limit to his understanding.

PSALM 147:5

Have you ever felt like no one understood you? No one knows what it's like to be you. No one knows how you feel about things. No one can get down inside your brain and be you for a few minutes to understand.

Well, there is one who understands. That is God. He understands all about you. Your fears. Your worries. Your hopes. Your dreams. Your sins. Your good deeds. He understands all about you, and he loves you. That means when he understands you, he can always put you in the true and best light. He sees you for what you are.

That's why God is the best friend anyone can have. Is he your friend?

Thank you, Lord, for being my friend. I hope we can always be best friends, forever. In Jesus' name, amen.

THEME: THE GREATNESS OF GOD

Love Higher Than the Heavens

Great is your love. It is higher than the heavens. Your truth reaches to the skies.

PSALM 108:4

How great is God's love?

Great enough to create you in a unique, perfect way.

Great enough to watch you grow and protect you along the way.

Great enough to listen to you when you hurt. Great enough to answer your prayers, even before you made them.

Great enough to die for your sins. Great enough to make it possible for you to have eternal life.

Great enough to want you to be with him forever.

That's some love. Have you felt it? Have you tasted it? Have you let it change your life?

I want your love to be in my mind and heart every day, Lord. Don't let me ever forget how much you love my family and me. Amen.

THEME: THE GREATNESS OF GOD

Right Among Us

People of Zion, give a loud shout! Sing with joy! The Holy One of Israel is among you. And he is great.

ISAIAH 12:6

In the Old Testament, God sometimes came down to visit his people. He appeared in different forms. For instance, in Abraham's day, he appeared with two angels to talk to Abraham and warn him about some things that were about to happen.

In Moses' day, God appeared on Mt. Sinai , in lightning and thunder. Then he led the people out of Egypt by appearing as a pillar of cloud by day and a pillar of fire by night.

The prophet Isaiah was carried up to God's very throne. He saw God "lifted up, with smoke filling the temple." God was majestic and marvelous to look at.

And then God appeared as Jesus. He is the final picture God gave us of himself. If you study Jesus, you will see an amazing portrait of God.

Are you studying him? Are you learning about him? He is the greatest one to study. And he rewards us for simply learning about him.

Teach me to sit at Jesus' feet and learn, to really soak in your words, Lord. Amen.

THEME: THE GREATNESS OF GOD

Faithful Forever

Great is his love for us. The LORD is faithful forever. Praise the LORD.

PSALM 117:2

There is a story about a man who kept a dog named Bobby. The dog became his loyal companion and was always with him. When the man died and was buried in Greyfriars Churchyard in Edinburgh, Scotland, Bobby stayed there by his grave day and night. He became known as Greyfriars Bobby. The only time he left the grave was to visit the local cook at a restaurant, and also the man who built a shelter for him in the graveyard. Greyfriars Bobby stayed by his master's grave for over five years, until his own death. When he died, the authorities buried him next to his master.

Dogs are known for their loyalty. So is God. God will stick with you forever. He will never give up on you, never cast you aside. Look to him and trust him, and you will never be friendless.

I hope I can be as loyal to you, Father, as you are to me. But if I'm not, I know you'll still be loyal, and that's great assurance. Amen.

THEME: THE GREATNESS OF GOD

Filled to the Brim with God's Love

May the Lord fill your hearts with God's love. May Christ give you the strength to go on.

2 THESSALONIANS 3:5

One of the things the apostle Paul most wanted us to understand is God's love. But how do you understand someone who

> created the universe knowing it would go bad?
> gave humankind hope instead of death after his sin?
> repeatedly gave people second chances?
> assured everyone that he had it all worked out?
> All we needed to do was trust him?
> sent his Son to die for us before we were even interested?

Yes, God's love is amazing, incredible, fantastic. But most of all, it's perfect. For all that love, do you think you can love him in return today?

Your love overwhelms me, eternal God. It is high. It is wide. It is more than I can ever understand. Thank you. Thank you. Thank you. Amen.

Wait for His Mercy

The mercy of our Lord Jesus Christ will bring you eternal life. As you wait for his mercy, remain in God's love.
JUDE 21

The most astonishing thing about God's love is that it keeps on going. Like the Energizer Bunny, he just keeps on loving.

Even when we sin.

Even when we sin the same sin for the thirtieth time.

Even when we're angry at him and want nothing to do with him.

Even when we're running as hard as we can away from him.

Even when we're filled with hatred.

God knows love will overcome the evil in our souls. Love him, and he'll love you a million times stronger in return.

Make my love for you shine as brightly as your love for me, Jesus. Amen.

THEME: GOD CARES FOR ME

Danger Ahead!

Anyone whose name was not written in the Book of Life was thrown into the lake of fire.

REVELATION 20:15

God's love runs out on some people.

Did you know that? There comes a day for everyone, when, if they keep pushing God away, God says, "So be it!"

God won't pursue us forever. God won't let us go on sinning forever. Those who hate and reject him, he will one day deal with permanently.

Here, in this passage, we see the end of Christ's rejecters. Because they never believed, their names are not written in the Book of Life. That's God's book that records everyone who has ever believed. The unbelievers are thrown into the Lake of Fire. We don't know all that the Lake of Fire does, but we know it won't be fun. Hell is a horrid place of darkness, hatred, and pain. It's the place where God sends those who hate him.

I pray for all those who don't know you tonight, Father. May you work in their hearts so many will know you tomorrow. Amen.

THEME: GOD CARES FOR ME

Your Name on His Hands

I have written your name on the palms of my hands. Your walls are never out of my sight.

ISAIAH 49:16

Did you know that your name is written on God's hands? According to this verse, that's exactly what he has done. You're tattooed there.

Think of how often you look at your hands. How often do you notice any grime or dirt there? Plenty of times.

God is saying here that he is continually reminded about you. Every time he looks at his hands, you're there. I wonder if he smiles, too. And thinks something nice about each of us.

The fact is, God thinks good things about all of us all of the time. He is positive about his love for us. He never gets negative.

Why don't you take your hands today and think of God every time you look at them?

I like the idea that my name is written on your hand, Lord. Do you look at it often? Thank you for remembering me. In Jesus, amen.

THEME: GOD CARES FOR ME

At My Right Hand

I know that the LORD is always with me. He is at my right hand. I will always be secure.

PSALM 16:8

Ned looked up at his new friend, Dean. They were both in fifth grade. But Dean was big for his age, with strong, hard muscles. Ned said to his friend, "We shouldn't walk around behind the shopping center. Some kids hang out there who beat up other kids."

"I'm not afraid," Dean said.

"Then I guess I'm not either," Ned said, "as long as you're with me."

They walked around behind the shopping center. Sure enough, several kids hung out back there, smoking and joking. When they saw Ned, they started to taunt him. But then they saw Dean. Everyone became silent at once.

Did you know that you have a friend like Dean? Jesus. He's with you wherever you are. That's a pretty good reason not to be afraid of anyone.

I don't want to be afraid of _____, Lord. But he scares me. Will you give me courage to face him? In Jesus, amen.

THEME: GOD CARES FOR ME

His Name on Our Foreheads

They will see his face. His name will be on their foreheads.
REVELATION 22:4

When Joy turned eleven and got into sixth grade, she realized her friend Nikki was a little different from other kids. Nikki was goofy. Sometimes she acted dumb. Occasionally, she did something outrageous.

But in time Joy realized Nikki was a good friend: loyal, kind, and giving. She decided that she didn't care what everyone said and she was proud to be Nikki's friend.

Sometimes people are like that about God. He's different. But he's your best friend and he's loyal, kind, and giving. So who cares what others say?

God is proud we're on his team. And he's so glad that we're his, that he intends to put his name on our foreheads. Someday, everyone will know the instant they meet us that we belong to him.

I can't wait to see your face, Jesus. Thank you for claiming me for yourself. Amen.

THEME: GOD CARES FOR ME

Death for God's Beloved

The LORD pays special attention when his faithful people die.

PSALM 116:15

Everyone is afraid of death sometime or other. They're afraid that it will hurt. And they're afraid of what happens afterwards.

For Christians, God assures us there's no reason to be afraid, either of dying or the aftermath. In another translation, the verse above says, "Precious in the sight of God is the death of his godly ones." What that means is that God pays close and special attention when we die. He knows how afraid we are. He understands that we don't want to die.

But God is there the whole time. He takes our hands. He whispers to us in our darkness. And he walks with us through the whole circumstance.

Don't be afraid of death. Know that God has it all planned and prepared and we are precious to him.

I know Jesus died for me on the cross, Lord, but help me to understand this better. It seems far away sometimes. In him, amen.

THEME: GOD CARES FOR ME

God So Loved the World That He Gave ...

God loved the world so much that he gave his one and only Son. Anyone who believes in him will not die but will have eternal life.

"How much do you love me?" Karen asked her toddler brother.

He held out his arms as far as they would go. "This much!" he shouted.

"And how much do you love Mama?"

Same answer.

"And Papa?"

Same answer again.

It's a fun game. It gets across the fact that we love someone more than we can calculate.

God didn't love us like that. He didn't just say, "I love you this much!" and hold out his hands. No, he showed us his love by sending Jesus to die for our sins. "What greater love does anyone have than to die for his friend?" Jesus once asked.

There can be no greater love. And that's how much God loved you!

God so loved me that he sent his Son. That's enough for me, Lord. Sign me up. Amen.

THEME: SALVATION

The Sins of the Whole World

He gave his life to pay for our sins. But he not only paid for our sins. He also paid for the sins of the whole world.

1 JOHN 2:2

How many sins did Jesus die for?

All of them. From the first in the Garden of Eden, to the last at the end of the book of Revelation.

How many people did Jesus die for?

All of them. From Adam and Eve to the last sinner at the end of history.

How many of us does Jesus love?

All of us. From the worst to the best. From the smallest to the tallest.

Jesus holds out his hand to us. He tells us he came to give us life. All we need to do is believe. How can anyone reject such love?

I know Jesus will keep me to the end, Lord. But all I'm asking right now is that he keep me through today. In his name, amen.

THEME: SALVATION

Not Judged

Those who believe in him are not judged. But those who do not believe are judged already. They have not believed in the name of God's one and only Son.

JOHN 3:18

Paul lay on his bed looking up at the ceiling. His brother asked, "What's the matter?"

"I'm thinking about God's judgment."

"Are you scared?" his brother asked.

"Yeah," Paul answered. "What if I have to pay for all the bad things I've done?"

I would be scared too, if I wasn't a Christian. But Christians need never fear God's judgment. Why? Because God has already judged us by judging Jesus. Jesus has already paid for the bad things we've done.

If we believe, we will never be judged in a negative sense. Instead, God will "judge" us to reward us for what we did in this life. And that judgment is a good judgment, one to look forward to.

I'm not afraid of you, Lord, because you love me. How can anyone be afraid of someone who loves them? In Jesus I pray, amen.

THEME: SALVATION

The Savior of All People

We have put our hope in the living God. He is the Savior of all people. Most of all he is the Savior of those who believe.
1 TIMOTHY 4:10

Rebecca listened to the teacher intently. She had said, "Jesus is everyone's Savior."

Rebecca raised her hand. "I'm not a Christian, Mrs. Evans. But you're saying Jesus died for me, too?"

"Yes, he did, Rebecca."

"And my whole family? My parents and sisters?"

"All of them."

"My uncles and aunts? And my cousins too?"

"Yes, Rebecca. The whole world."

"Then I guess I'd better believe in him."

"Believe even if the others don't, Rebecca. It's up to each of us to believe, regardless of what anyone else does."

That's the way God deals with the world. It's one on one, one by one. You can't believe for anyone else. But you can believe for you.

Have you believed? Are you sure? Are you letting him change your life?

Thank you that you save everyone, Jesus, but thank you especially for saving me. Amen.

THEME: SALVATION

God Wants All of Them

*The Lord is not slow to keep his promise. He is not slow
in the way some people understand it. He is patient with
you. He doesn't want anyone to be destroyed. Instead, he
wants all people to turn away from their sins.*

2 PETER 3:9

Jesus is coming back.

But for 2000 years, he has not come back. Some say
that's proof he will never come back. Why does God
delay? Why doesn't he make it happen today?

For a simple reason: he wants to give everyone possible a chance to believe. He's "not slow to keep his
promise," as the Scripture says. He's patient. He's waiting. He's biding his time. So that everyone will get a
chance to hear the gospel and believe.

If someone says to you, "Jesus is never coming back.
If he was, he would have by now," tell them, "Maybe
he's just waiting for you to believe!"

It's possible!

*I want Jesus to come back soon, Lord. But if he doesn't,
I still want to be faithful. Amen.*

THEME: SALVATION

Live by Faith

The one who is right with God will live by faith.

HABAKKUK 2:4

How do we live?

By money? Yes, we need money to live. But we don't live by it. We live off of it. We live with it. But we don't live because of it.

By eating food? Certainly. But we don't live because of food. If we do, we'll probably gain so much weight, we'll have to be carried around in a stretcher!

No, there's only one way to live: by faith.

What does it mean to live by faith? It means that your life is sustained and continues because you trust in and believe in Jesus. The only thing that keeps you alive is faith. Without faith, you're in great danger. Any moment you could be taken away. And then there is nothing left but your soul. Which has no faith.

Only faith can make us clean in God's sight. Only faith enables us to be good and right in God's eyes. Why? Because our faith is in Jesus who was clean and good and right for us.

Are you living by faith?

I'm glad Jesus not only paid for my sins, Father, but also lived a perfect life in my place. Amen.

THEME: SALVATION

Serve!

Be like the Son of Man. He did not come to be served. Instead, he came to serve others. He came to give his life as the price for setting many people free.

MATTHEW 20:28

"Well, now I've joined the church," Rachel said to her pastor. "What do I do now?"

"The same thing Jesus did," said her pastor.

"What was that?"

"Serve. Jesus came to serve."

Imagine if the whole world decided it would serve others as its primary duty. What would happen?

People would be polite, mannerly.

No one would sin against another.

Everyone would be ready to help, in any situation.

The gospel would go to the ends of the earth.

The world would be a friendlier, kinder place.

If you decide to serve today, you've made the world a step closer to Jesus' goal for our planet. Serve, and don't give up. God will reward you.

Let me serve the way Jesus did, Lord. Let me serve wherever and whenever. Amen.

THEME: SALVATION

Son of David, Son of Abraham

This is the record of the family line of Jesus Christ. He is the son of David. He is also the son of Abraham.

MATTHEW 1:1

In Matthew 1, we find the ancestors of Jesus listed. It's an amazing list. There are good people and bad people on this list. There are several women who were complete outcasts. There are kings who were so wicked, God himself had to destroy them. And there are King David and Abraham, the two leading members of the list.

Who was King David? The greatest king of Israel. But at one point in his life he committed a terrible sin and everything turned against him.

Then there is Abraham, the founder of the Jews. He lied, he failed to believe God at times, and he almost messed up God's plan for his family.

What are these men signs of? God's grace. If God can use these people and even put them in Jesus' line, what do you think he can do with you?

I'm glad everyone in the Bible wasn't perfect, Jesus. I can learn from them, and also beware of doing what they did! Amen.

THEME: THE BIRTH OF JESUS

A Christmas to Remember

Do not be afraid, Mary. God is very pleased with you. You will become pregnant and give birth to a son. You must name him Jesus. He will be great and will be called the Son of the Most High God.

LUKE 1:30–32

Today is Christmas Day. We remember Jesus' birth this day, even though it may not have been his actual birthday! Fact is, we don't know what day Jesus was born on. December 25th is a date the church decided to use, even though they didn't have proof.

Still, it's a good day to remember. But remember what? That God came into the world, a little baby like all of us. God came by a peasant woman. God came in the form of a child. He came as a poor son. But he was the Son of God. He was the one whose birth we would remember as the turning point of history.

As you open gifts today, remember him who came. Why? For you.

It's Christmas again, Lord, and I'm excited. Help me to remember, though, that you're behind it all. In Jesus, amen.

THEME: THE BIRTH OF JESUS

Born of a Virgin

Joseph, son of David, don't be afraid to take Mary home as your wife. The baby inside her is from the Holy Spirit.

MATTHEW 1:20

Sometimes people say odd things about Jesus. Like that he couldn't have been born of a virgin. What's a virgin? It's a woman who has never had sexual relations with a man. Only through sex can a woman conceive a baby.

Normally, that is.

But Jesus was born *of* a virgin. God was his Father. He wasn't *normal*, in that sense. He was the most abnormal person ever born. How come?

Because he was perfect.

Because he was sinless.

Because he was the Son of God.

Because he would save the world.

Because of all those things, he deserves our utmost worship.

Let me worship you today, Father. Here are three things I'm thankful for: _____, _____, and _____. Amen.

THEME: THE BIRTH OF JESUS

No Room at the Inn

She gave birth to her first baby. It was a boy. She wrapped him in large strips of cloth. Then she placed him in a manger. There was no room for them in the inn.

LUKE 2:7

Have you ever been traveling with your family late at night, with no place to stay?

On my honeymoon, my wife and I planned to stop in St. Louis one night. But when we got there, the first hotel we stopped at was full. So was the second. And the third, fourth, fifth. There was no room at the inn. I was scared. I was tired. I wanted to sleep.

Finally, we found a dingy little place far outside St. Louis. The room was hot. It smelled. It was tiny. But it was a place to stay. I was relieved.

Jesus' family didn't even have that. They had a stable. Think of staying overnight there!

But Jesus did it. Why? So no one anywhere could say he had it easy. Everyone could know he understands what it's like to be in their situation.

Do you think he understands yours?

I'm glad Jesus didn't have it great when he lived on earth, Lord. That makes me feel better when I don't have it so great. In him, amen.

Great News from Above

Do not be afraid. I bring you good news of great joy. It is for all the people. Today in the town of David a Savior has been born to you. He is Christ the Lord.

LUKE 2:10–11

Angels spoke these words to shepherds sitting out with their flocks in the hills above Bethlehem. Shepherds were rough men. The people of Israel regarded shepherds as losers who could do nothing better with their lives than watch sheep.

Isn't it amazing that God announced his Son's birth to shepherds? Why not to the city of Bethlehem? Why not to King Herod?

It's as if God was saying, "These are the people who most need a Savior. I'm telling them they have hope. Hope they never had before."

God has a special place in his heart for the poor, homeless, lost, young, neglected, and hurting. And that includes you!

I praise you, Jesus, that you came as a baby, in a stable, announced to shepherds. I just wish I had been there to see you. In Jesus, amen.

THEME: THE BIRTH OF JESUS

The Wise Men

The Wise Men ... bowed down and worshiped him. Then they opened their treasures. They gave him gold, incense and myrrh.

MATTHEW 2:11

Who were the wise men?

They were men who studied the stars and read messages into their patterns. They lived in the East, probably Persia. They were descended from "magi" in the court of Babylon. If you look in Daniel 2:48, you'll find an interesting thing: Daniel, a Jew, was in charge of the "wise men."

Then what happened? Undoubtedly, Daniel told these men about the prophecies of the prophets of Israel. One of those prophecies told of a star (see Numbers 24:17) that would come from Jacob. This star would be the sign of the coming of Israel's Messiah.

The wise men passed on this message from generation to generation. Finally, they saw the star and came to Israel looking for the new king. Their faith had lived through many generations, and now it was satisfied.

Have you put your faith in the boy born under that star? If you have, you are a "wise man" indeed!

Help me to be wise and believe in you, Jesus. Amen.

THEME: THE BIRTH OF JESUS

The One That Takes Away Sin

Look! The Lamb of God! He takes away the sin of the world!

JOHN 1:29

John the Baptist spoke these words when he saw Jesus. He called Jesus the "Lamb of God." Why did he do that?

In the worship system of Israel, Jews gave sacrifices. These sacrifices were usually animals or birds. The sacrifices represented different things, but a primary sacrifice was for sin. When an animal was brought to the temple as a sacrifice, the Jewish believer laid his hands on its head. The priest spoke some words. Immediately, a transfer took place. In the eyes of God, that Jew's sins were put on that animal. Then it was killed in the Jew's place. Lambs were one of the favorite animals to sacrifice. They represented innocence, beauty, and simplicity.

All those sacrifices pointed to Jesus. He would come and be the final sacrifice for sins. He paid the price of death that we might live.

I thank you, Lord, for the awesome sacrifice of your life on the cross. Amen.

THEME: THE BIRTH OF JESUS

Toward a New Year

Teach us to realize how short our lives are. Then our hearts will become wise.

PSALM 90:12

The new year is dawning. Only a few hours left. Why not take a moment and review this past year? Answer a few questions?

What stands out in your memory as a high point? A low point?

Are there any things in the last year of which you're proud? Or ashamed?

Did you learn anything new and precious about Jesus? Or God? Or the Bible?

Did you use your time for good things? Or bad things?

Is there anyone you need to get right with? Patch up a bad relationship? Apologize for something you did to them?

God wants us to take a look at our lives frequently. Why? So we'll become wise. Looking back is the best thing next to looking ahead, and up!

It's the end of a year, the beginning of a new year. Let this be the year I serve you better than I ever have before. In Jesus, amen.

THEME: LOOKING BACK

Index of Old Testament Readings

Index of Old Testament Readings

Index of New Testament Readings

Index of New Testament Readings

Index of New Testament Readings

Index of New Testament Readings

Index of New Testament Readings

Index of Themes

We want to hear from you. Please send your comments
about this book to us in care of zreview@zondervan.com. Thank you.

ZONDERVAN.com/
AUTHORTRACKER
follow your favorite authors